WITHDRAWN
L. R. COLLEGE LIBRARY

S0-ACK-589

WITHDRAWN
L. R. COLLEGE LIBRARY

PENN

by
Elizabeth Janet Gray

ILLUSTRATED BY GEORGE GILLETT WHITNEY

Philadelphia Yearly Meeting
of the Religious Society of Friends
Philadelphia, Pennsylvania

CARL A. RUDISILL LIBRARY
LENOIR-RHYNE COLLEGE

About the Author

ELIZABETH GRAY VINING was born in Philadelphia shortly after the turn of the century. She was graduated from Bryn Mawr College, and in the years that followed, under the names Elizabeth Janet Gray and Elizabeth Gray Vining, she wrote many books for adults and children, including the Newbery Award winner *Adam of the Road*.

During and immediately after World War II, Mrs. Vining worked for the American Friends Service Committee. In 1946 she was appointed tutor to Crown Prince Akihito of Japan and later wrote the widely read *Windows for the Crown Prince*. She is the author of several novels and biographies, and her autobiography, *Quiet Pilgrimage*, was published in 1970.

Elizabeth Gray Vining lives southwest of Philadelphia, in Kennett Square, Pennsylvania.

Also by Elizabeth Janet Gray
Sandy, Adam of the Road, The Fair Adventure, Beppy Marlowe,
Young Walter Scott, Jane Hope, Meggy MacIntosh
The Cheerful Heart, I Will Adventure

F
152.2
.V 78
1986
1 5 9864
Sept. 1953

© 1938 by Elizabeth Janet Gray
All rights reserved

A hardcover edition of this book
was originally published by the Viking Press, 1938
with printings
1941, 1944, 1947, 1950, 1953, 1955, 1957, 1960, 1962, 1963

Published 1986
by the Philadelphia Yearly Meeting
of the Religious Society of Friends
1515 Cherry Street, Philadelphia, Pennsylvania 19102

Printed in the United States of America
by Graphics Standard, West Chester, Pennsylvania 19380

Library of Congress Catalog Number 86-63992
ISBN: 0-941308-06-5

LIBRARY
LENOIR-RHYNE COLLEGE

Contents

Contents

Illustrations

Illustrations

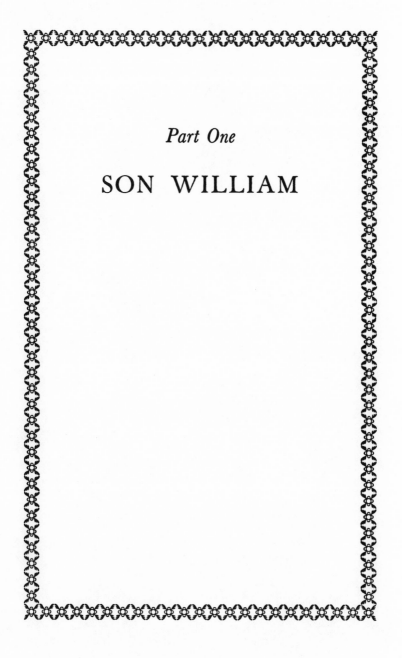

Part One

SON WILLIAM

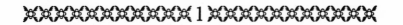

Captain Penn Hurries Home

THE *Fellowship* was about to sail. The stretch of the Thames called Limehouse Reach was full of shipping this October morning: barges and lighters bearing goods, wherries darting in and out like water bugs, fishing-boats from Holland with square brown sails, vessels whose tall masts and rigging pricked the sky above the pointed roofs and clustered chimney pots of the houses along the Deptford shore, and the great warships of the English Navy bristling with guns and swarming with sailors in red breeches and blue jackets.

Young Captain Penn, handsome, round-faced, fair-haired, stood on his quarterdeck. He was just twenty-three. This was his first command, and he was proud of his *Fellowship* of Bristol, proud of every stout oak timber, every one of her twenty-eight guns, her hundred and ten seamen. Great of draft she might be, and unwieldy, but she was his; with her he was setting forth to defend the western ports of England and Wales against King Charles's forces, and to protect the Protestants in Ireland from the Roman Catholic rebellion raging there.

And that, thought Captain Penn, was doing not too badly, at twenty-three. His father had urged him, when

3

he married last January, to withdraw from the Navy and undertake a mercantile voyage to the Levant to make his fortune, but he had refused outright. No doubt his father, Captain Giles Penn, knew the sea and knew the world, but he, William, knew his own mind and would steer his own course. And was he not already a captain?

The first sunshine of the morning gleamed suddenly on the polished masts, the white sails; it settled luminously into the pale mist that curled up from the silver surface of the Thames; it made young Captain Penn crinkle up his blue eyes. It shone on the crowded river and, beyond the river, on London, a mass of huddled roofs between the Tower and the Temple.

The sails bellied out and took the light breeze; the seamen stamped and sang as they wound up the anchor; the capstan creaked; the *Fellowship* lifted a little beneath her captain's feet, and the shores began to move, Deptford on the right and the Isle of Dogs on the left.

Captain Penn looked back at London. He could see the four turrets of the Tower. He could almost believe that he saw the roof of the little house on Tower Hill where he had said good-by to Margaret—gay, warm-hearted, untidy, happy-go-lucky Margaret, who had been his wife since January last. They were poor now, most inconveniently so, but they would not be poor long. They had expectations. Margaret's Irish estates would pay again one day, and he would rise in the Navy. He would be so good a captain that even though England was torn with civil war, the Parliament against the King,

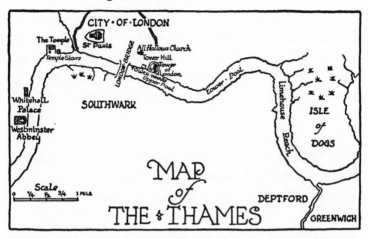

he would rise in the service of the Navy. They would have much to give their child. Captain Penn would be an admiral, but his son—if God willed that it be a son—would go higher still.

The *Fellowship* dropped down the river.

Some time later, we do not know exactly when, the message came. The *Fellowship* put about. Back she sailed up Woolwich Reach, up Blackwall Reach, past Greenwich, and anchored once again among the boats off Deptford. The young captain, in a very ferment, left his ship and took a wherry, one of those little boats rowed by stout oarsmen that plied up and down the Thames, carrying folk from the Tower Wharf to Milford Stairs, from the City to Westminster, or wherever else they wished to go.

Captain Penn was landed at the Tower Wharf early

on the morning of October 14. Up the hill he hurried in the chilly shadow of the Tower wall to the house where he and Margaret lived in two rooms, one above the other. He made all possible haste, but even before he reached the door, he heard the thin cry of the newborn child.

It was a boy.

So for the first time, they saw each other—Captain William Penn and "Son William," those two who were to love each other deeply and oppose each other strenuously.

Nine days later they baptized the baby in the little ancient church near by, called All Hallows, Barking, and soon after that the captain was off once more, leaving the baby and his mother alone together.

The year was 1644. The King and his court had been obliged by the Roundheads to withdraw to Oxford, and he had taken with him his two sons—Charles, fourteen, and James, eleven. Away in Leicestershire, in the lonely places, a twenty-year-old shoemaker and shepherd named George Fox, who found no comfort in the religions that caused civil war, walked many nights by himself, waiting for the Lord to speak. In London an eight-month-old baby girl, Gulielma Springett, took her daily ride through the quiet paths of Lincoln's Inn Fields in her carriage drawn by her footman. And more than three thousand miles over the ocean red Indians hunted deer and wild turkeys in a vast tract of forest land, owned by the Dutch, that lay between the Puritan settlements of

New England on the north and Lord Baltimore's Roman Catholic colony to the south.

And all these scattered lives were to play their part in the life of the baby who slept and cried and ate and slept again in sight of the steep walls of the old, grim Tower, into which had gone, down the centuries, many prisoners, young and old, frightened and defiant; and from which fewer had come out. The Tower too had its part.

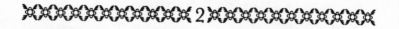

2

While the West Wind Blew

T HE wind blew out of the west on that twenty-ninth
day of July 1653, a raw, chilly wind bringing clouds
and scudding rain. It lashed at the old trees in Hainault
Forest and strewed the ground underneath with green
leaves and bits of branches. It tugged at the long coat of
young William Penn, who was on his way to school before six o'clock in the morning with his Lily's *Latin
Grammar* and Cleonard's *Greek Grammar* under his arm.
He was hurrying, for he was almost late, and the wind
made going difficult, swelling his coat out behind him as
it did and then suddenly veering around and flapping it
back against his legs. He was a handsome lad, tall for a
boy not yet nine, and well built. People said he looked
like his father.

He was thinking, as he trudged along bent into the
wind, that you could not hear the guns today. When the
wind was in the east, the pound of the guns in the English Channel blew all the way across the Essex marshes,
and William, hearing that distant thunder and roar,
would think of his father, who was out there fighting
the Dutch. He was proud of his father, who was Vice-
Admiral of the English fleet and who had gone out to

Van Tromp's broom

fight that Dutchman, Van Tromp, who had tied a broom to his main top mast and said he would sweep English shipping out of the Channel. He was proud of his father, but he felt better—and so did his mother—when he could not hear the guns.

But today the wind was in the west. It came whistling over London, eleven miles away, where William had been born and where he had lived when he was very small, where King Charles I was executed and Oliver Cromwell and the Parliament ruled in his place, where the Tower loomed up beside the Thames, and where his father's ships sometimes came to anchor. Now and then on special occasions the Penns' servant would ride to London to get a venison pasty from the pie-shop in Fetter Lane, or William's mother would go to buy silk for William's Sunday suit at the 'Change and fine cambric for little Pegg's white caps. When the west wind blew over London, it brought clouds with it, but the guns were silent.

As he came to the edge of the little village of Chigwell, he heard the bell begin to ring, the bell which Archbishop Harsnett, who had founded the Grammar School, had given in his will, with twenty shillings a year to the clerk who rang it. William paused a moment at the top of the hill. From here on a clear day you could see all the way to London. Today all he could see was the little village plunging down the hill below him, with the school and the inn and the church at its foot, and a gray-green sea of tossing woods beyond.

He began to run, taking the slope in great leaps, his coat blowing out behind him. He loved to run. Footracing was the great sport in Essex—young William thought it the greatest sport in the world—and already he was making a name for himself among the fleet of foot.

He was at the school gate before the bell stopped ringing; he had come down so fast that he skidded and almost fell when he pulled up short to go into the yard. Most of the boys lived at the school and were already inside, but a few day-scholars like William were hurrying across the yard to the two "fair and large" buildings that housed the English and the Latin schools. Fine stone buildings they were, too, with red-tiled roofs and everything very modern, being less than twenty-five years old.

William went through the door into the Latin school and got to his place in the big form-room just in time to kneel down and join with all the low husky voices repeating the Lord's Prayer and the *Te Deum Laudamus*.

Then the long school day settled in with a rustle and a sigh, in the big room that was rain-dim and chilly, for all it was almost the first of August by the calendar. It was Friday, and that meant that they worked straight through from six to eleven, and then from one until six came around again. On Thursdays and Saturdays, in summer, they had an hour off in the morning and another in the afternoon, to play. In winter they started at seven every day and studied till five.

William opened his Tully. Tully and Terence they read for phrase and style, the master said. For poetry they would read, when they were older, Homer and Vergil. That was Archbishop Harsnett's own plan for his school; his boys were to have plenty of the ancient Greek and Latin writers, but no "conceited modern writers," no novelties by Shakespeare or Milton. William wondered sometimes about Shakespeare, who had written plays. Plays were forbidden under the Commonwealth, but William's mother had seen one when she was young, and she said it was mighty divertising.

The bench on which William sat was hard. His legs grew stiff, and his back began to ache. If only he could get up and stretch, or go outdoors and run. Tomorrow was Saturday, and the next day was Sunday. Perhaps on Sunday they would drive over to Walthamstow to see Sir William Batten, and he could play in the garden with the five girls or walk in the great vinery. Sir William had been his father's admiral in the days of his duty in the Irish Sea and was now retired. He knew all about the sea and ships, he even knew the *James*, which was Father's own ship, of seventy guns and nearly a thousand tons. He could tell young William how the fleet was divided into three squadrons, how his father was commander of the white squadron, and how, when he wanted the captains of his ships to come on board the *James* for a conference, he would hang a white flag in his mizzen shrouds and fire one gun. William loved to talk with Sir William Batten; they both knew that Vice-Admiral Penn was a great man.

He saw the master looking at him, and turned a page hastily. The master was exactly the kind of man that the Archbishop had prescribed in his rules for the school: "a good poet, of a sound religion, of a sober and honest conversation; no puffer of tobacco; and above all apt to teach and severe in his government."

At eleven the boys were released for two hours to eat their dinner and play in the yard. The big boys took up most of the room, so that the little ones were herded into corners; but sometimes, as today, it occurred to the older ones that it would be fun to hold a race for the youngsters. So they lined up all the small fry, starting them off, shouting for their favorites, and deciding which was the winner. Young William Penn loved it. He took off his long coat and ran in his shirt and breeches, and he easily outdistanced the others, both running and jumping the hurdles. When he went back to school again at one o'clock, his shirt was clinging to his shoulders, his cheeks were glowing, and all the kinks were out of his legs.

The afternoon session was endless. They had a whole page of rules in Lily's *Grammar* to get by heart, and every boy must drone out every rule before the master was satisfied. The hours from one to six dragged slowly past. At the close of the day they said the hundred and thirteenth psalm—always the same one, though William thought there were others just as good and more interesting.

"From the rising of the sun unto the going down of the same, the Lord's name is to be praised," said the master.

And as the boys responded with the next verse William thought: How could they praise the Lord's name when they were in school from the rising of the sun to the going down of the same, all that time getting by heart pages of Latin grammar? He was tired as he gathered up his books, so very tired, and hungry. It had been a day just like any other day, except that there had been no sound of guns from the Channel. The west wind whistled still around the school house.

He did not know that on this day a great fight at sea had been begun, that the English fleet had met the Dutch

at the mouth of the Texel, and that all day long the
guns had been thundering and hurling forth death and
would not stop tomorrow or the next day, till thirty
Dutch ships were sunk, and proud and brave Admiral
Van Tromp was dead with a musket ball in his chest.

Within the next few days all the villages, Chigwell
and Wanstead and Walthamstow, were ringing with the
news. It came in bits. General Monk had written a report to the Council of State, and so had Vice-Admiral
Penn. A hasty note which had come to Mrs. Penn from
the Admiral, saying that he was safe and that it had been
a great day, was shown and passed about till it was all
but worn out. Nobody could talk of anything else; it was
tantalizing to have so few facts. It was said that General
Blake and General Monk and Vice-Admiral Penn and
Rear-Admiral Lawson were all to have gold chains and
medals made by Mr. Simon the goldsmith to remember
the day. It was said that Vice-Admiral Penn and Major-
General Desborough were to be made Generals of the
Fleet along with Monk and Blake.

Parliament set aside a day of thanksgiving, and ordered that the full account of the battle was to be read in
all the churches, which was the only satisfactory way to
get the news to everyone.

William and his mother went to the thanksgiving
service in the church at Chigwell. William wore his best
suit of ash-colored silk with a lace collar and cuffs, and a
green scarf to hold his sword. Mrs. Penn was wearing
her best clothes too, and very smiling and proud she

looked. She and William agreed that it was a pity little Pegg was only a baby, too young to understand what a great day this was, or to remember it. They had left her playing with her alphabetical bricks, with her cap pulled around till it was over one eye in the most rakish way imaginable. They sat in the center of the church, and the Grammar School boys marched two by two into the gallery above. William felt their eyes on him. He felt everybody's eyes on him—and the church was crowded. Wasn't he the son of the great Admiral?

He forgot himself when the congregation began to sing the *Te Deum*. It sounded altogether different from the way it sounded at school. No mumbling today. The people shouted it out with a joyful voice.

The vicar read from the pulpit the official account of what he called England's greatest sea-battle. William did not hear the numbers of Dutch ships taken and Dutch sailors killed. He was thinking of his father, his brave and handsome father, tall and blue-eyed, commanding yet jolly looking. He was thinking that his father was the greatest man in the whole world.

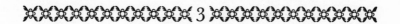

3

The General Goes to the Tower

A YEAR later, at the fall of the leaf, the Penns were back on Great Tower Hill, not in their old cramped quarters but in a house on the east side within a court adjoining London Wall. General Penn, whom Oliver Cromwell, now Lord Protector of England, had appointed commander-in-chief of the fleet and sea-forces of an expedition to take Hispaniola from the Spaniards, had to go to London to equip the fleet, and he took his family with him. General Penn was now a great man indeed. Everybody said so, and when he wanted to make his family secure, in case he should not return from the West Indies, he had only to remind Oliver that Mrs. Penn's Irish estates had suffered losses in the late rebellion, and Oliver at once ordered that he should be given Irish lands worth three hundred pounds a year, "with a castle or convenient house for habitation, and near to some town or garrison"—and this as much for "his good and faithful services to the Commonwealth" as for the losses his wife's estates had sustained.

Great was the stir and bustle within the house on Tower Hill. General Penn had forty ships to equip and make ready, all their stores and supplies to get, and many

"Sometimes he took young William with him"

of their officers to select. He had to think of everything from captains down to water casks and a particular kind of loadstone for the compasses. He went over every detail again and again, for this was the most important command of his whole life—and though he was only thirty-three, he had seen fighting in the Irish Sea, in the Mediterranean, and, sharpest of all, in the narrow waters of the English Channel. All day there was coming and going at all hours, men with messages, men with things to sell, captains who came to confer with him, and generals too—General Venables, who was to command the land-army of six regiments of foot that was going with them, and General Desborough, who was one of the commissioners of the admiralty. So many men came to apply for posts in the fleet that there was not room to see them all in the house, and he had to arrange to interview those below the rank of commander out of doors on Tower Hill near the house.

Sometimes he took young William with him, and the boy loved that. He liked being released from his private school and his tutor, and still better he liked the rare privilege of being with his father and seeing him so important among other men, a great man who did things that would be written about in history. He liked to see his father's way with the men; with all his dignity and power he was still easy and kindly, so that even those whom he sent away felt friendly toward him. A young man who applied for the position of purser-general and was turned down because he was not old enough, wrote of General Penn years later that he was "fair-haired; of a comely round visage; a mild-spoken man, no scoffer or flatterer; easy of access, so that no person went from him discontented."

So October went by, and November; it was mid-December before the fleet was ready. Then the six regiments of foot-soldiers marched to Portsmouth to embark. General Penn went to Portsmouth by coach, and Mrs. Penn went with him to see him off.

When she came back, she told young William all about it: how big and fine Father's own ship, the *Swiftsure*, looked, with the Admiral's flag flying; how General Venables was taking his wife with him, which everyone thought most imprudent, but there was no law against it; how on Christmas Day in the morning Mrs. Penn stood on the hill in a fresh east wind and saw the fleet riding the waters of the Spithead, flags flying and sails gleaming in the winter sunshine; how the *Swiftsure* loosed her fore top sail and fired one gun, and in answer to the signal all the ships weighed anchor, the *Golden Cock*, the *Little Charity*, the *Marigold*, the *Bear*, the *Gilliflower*, and all the others whose names she couldn't remember. She heard the trumpets blare out and then grow faint, and she saw the white ships grow smaller and smaller like a flock of sea-gulls flying away.

General Desborough went aboard the *Swiftsure* with General Penn and General Venables, but he came back with the pilot, bringing a letter from her husband to Mrs. Penn. He had nothing to write to her about, for he had left her but a few hours earlier, except his love and thought of her, but he sent her a letter because it would be his last chance for so long.

And that was all the story. "General Desborough saw me safe to Kingston, where we dined together," said William's mother, her voice gone a little flat, "and everyone returned to their homes."

There was one thing more, which she told almost absently. "The two coachmen were talking together, and one of the wheels raised up against a bank and overturned us. But no one was hurt, thanks be to the Lord. It was hard by Godalming."

And the while William sat thinking of the white sails

bending toward Hispaniola, where all the gold and silver was, and pineapples and parrots, his mother went to write a letter to his father. But no one knew when it would reach him.

They returned to Chigwell, Mrs. Penn and young William and Pegg and the tutor, and settled down to face the fact that war was not all flags and trumpets and Spanish prizes. It was gray winter days without news, and nights of anxiety and dread, and a house that seemed empty and forlorn because the head of it was away and might not come back at all.

It was March before they heard that the fleet had safely reached the English Island of Barbados, where they put in for supplies before attacking Hispaniola. The roses were in bloom and Hainault Forest was riotous with the songs of thrushes and blackbirds, before they knew that the attempt on Hispaniola had failed miserably.

People could hardly believe it. An English army repulsed by a few Spaniards! It was said that there were sickness and fever in the fleet, and that General Venables was hampered by the presence of his wife, but that hardly made the failure less ignominious. The Penns, aghast and bewildered, yet carried their heads high. If the land-army had failed, that was not the fault of the fleet. General Penn had set the six regiments ashore, he had waited under Spanish fire and taken the defeated soldiers on board again; what more could he have done?

By the end of July word had come that Jamaica had been captured instead, and that General Penn had led the way with his own ship. Some thought Jamaica was more valuable than Hispaniola.

In September General Penn and General Venables and nineteen ships of the fleet of forty came sailing home to explain to Cromwell and the Council, leaving the others to guard Jamaica.

The first rejoicing of the Penns was soon quenched. Disaster came swiftly. Three weeks after their return the two generals were in the Tower of London.

A dozen miles away in Chigwell a boy of eleven went about with his heart all but bursting with anger and pain for his hero.

His father was not long in the Tower, only five weeks, but it was long enough to make him begin to grow old at thirty-four. He went into the Tower a general of the fleet, the only real seaman ever to have won the title (all the others having been land generals first), and he came out plain Mr. Penn, stripped of his command, humiliated, broken in health and spirits—but free.

After the first relief and joy over having him home again had subsided, the household was a gloomy one. Young William Penn, doing his lessons with his tutor, running in the Forest in his free time, playing with little Pegg, had much to think about. He wondered what would happen to them all, and if his father would always be sad and silent, his mother worried. He wondered why such things happened, why God allowed a great man to be punished unjustly, and if there was a God anyhow.

Alone in his room one day, he had a strange experience.

Suddenly he knew there was a God, not because people said so in church, but because he knew it within his own heart. He felt as if God Himself were telling him so, and for a fleeting moment the room seemed to be filled with a holy light, and he felt comforted.

It was gone almost at once. He did not speak of it to anyone. Sometimes for long periods he did not even think of it, but he never quite forgot it. Years later he knew what it meant.

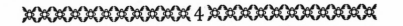

4

To Ireland!

WHATEVER else he had lost, William Penn, who had been General of the Fleet, still had his estates in Ireland which Cromwell had given him just before the Hispaniola expedition set forth and which he had never seen. As his spirits began to revive he thought of them, of his castle of Macroom, his garrison, and his farms, and soon he was making plans to move his whole family to the Province of Munster. But first they had to wait until the new baby, Dickie, arrived.

By the summer of 1656 the Penn household was again astir with preparations, and Admiral Penn must have thought that forty ships could be got ready for the West Indies with less commotion than one family with three children for Ireland. But it was a relief after all the heavy-hearted months to be looking hopefully into the future toward a new home and a new life. To Mrs. Penn it was a return to the country of her girlhood; to William, who had never traveled farther than from Chigwell to London and back, it was Adventure; it was Seeing the World.

Quite a troop set forth on the ship *Basing* on the twelfth of August: Admiral and Mrs. Penn; William; Pegg, who was five and as lively and curious as a kitten;

Dickie the baby, wound in his long clothes like a moth in a cocoon; William's tutor; the necessary women servants; and Jack, the black boy whom the Admiral had brought back from Jamaica. A parrot which General Venables had given him went too.

Another family traveling in some state was also on the *Basing*, Lord Broghill, the President of Munster, and his lady, and their servants. Lord Broghill and Admiral Penn had been friends for years, ever since William's father was a young captain on guard duty in Irish waters. My lord told William how he and young Captain Penn had sailed together on the *Fellowship* from the Spithead to Kinsale, and how the young captain had told him over and over that he had a baby son at home on Tower Hill.

They were three days at sea in hot and glistening August weather. William explored the ship thoroughly and talked to all the seamen, and after that, whenever he could escape from his tutor and from Pegg, one or the other of whom seemed to be eternally tagging after him, he liked to sit quiet and unnoticed on a stool or a coil of rope close by his father and Lord Broghill and hear them talk together. Occasionally when they forgot he was there, they spoke of the King, by whom they meant King Charles II, who was living in exile in Holland. Sometimes they spoke of the Quakers, a fanatical new religious sect which was growing so fast that people were frightened. Admiral Penn said that three years ago they had never been heard of in Bristol, and now there were more than a thousand of them in that city alone—an old

Penn listens to his father and Lord Broghill

friend of his had been convinced. Lord Broghill said that they had got a foothold in Ireland too; there were thirteen in jail in Cork and Limerick, ten of them soldiers who refused to fight. It seemed that Quakers thought it wrong to fight. Admiral Penn and Lord Broghill laughed.

Young William Penn sat on a coil of rope with the August sun glittering off the restless water into his eyes and the clean, cool air blowing in his face, and wondered about this curious set of people who thought it wrong to fight.

Early on the fourth morning they came into Cork Harbor. Under a sky full of tumbling gray clouds a clear purplish light lay over the soft green hills that sloped

down to the gray water. Sea-gulls wheeled and squawked
and swooped about the ship. Away at the end of the
harbor near the mouth of the river Lee the little city of
Cork pushed its stony way up the hill.

Macroom Castle was twenty-four miles west of Cork.
It had belonged to the Earl of Clancarty, who had been
commander-in-chief of the forces of the Roman Catholic
rebellion. When that had been put down with great
bloodshed and cruelty by the army of the Commonwealth, Oliver Cromwell took the earl's estates away
from him and gave them to Admiral Penn. A fine place it
was, too, the castle, town, and manor of Macroom, which
was also a garrison with a foot company and a troop of
horse permanently stationed there. The Irish rebels having been driven from the land (all who had not been
killed), the Admiral was planning to settle it anew with
Englishmen, and already he had arranged with various of
his kinsmen to come and be his tenants. He set to work
to make it into a real English estate, and to buy more
land as soon as he could to fill out his boundaries to his
satisfaction.

After they had been in Ireland for about a year, Mrs.
Penn made a flying visit to some friends in Bristol across
the Irish Channel. She came back full of her trip, and told
her family all about it in her lively gossipy way.

Captain George Bishop, she said, the Admiral's old
friend, had not only turned Quaker but had written a
book setting forth the new doctrine. She had just glanced
at it, but she thought it very strange; they had no priests

or ministers, and they cared nothing for churches; they met and worshiped God in a room or out of doors on a hillside, and anyone could preach if the spirit moved him, women as well as men. Some people said they were blasphemous. A Quaker named Naylor had had a hole bored in his tongue with a red-hot iron and was branded on the forehead with the letter B for blasphemer. In Cork as she came through on her way home, she saw people flocking after a man who had come there from the city of Oxford to preach Quakerism. A young man he was, in his twenties, dressed in a frieze coat and plain hat; he looked like a pleasant, sensible man. It seemed that wherever you turned you met a Quaker.

"The captain of the ship I took passage on was a Quaker too—mild and peaceable, yet he had authority," she said. "But in Bristol they call them monsters and other harsh names. And some folk here are hot against this man Loe who has come to Cork."

"Let us," said the Admiral suddenly, "be like the noble Bereans."

Nobody knew just what he meant; they sat polite and attentive, waiting.

"Son William, why were the Bereans noble?"

Son William did not know, and was set to search out the passage in the *Acts of the Apostles*. He read:

" 'These were more noble than those in Thessalonica in that they received the word with all readiness of mind and searched the scriptures daily whether those things were so.' "

"I propose that we have this man Loe here," said the
Admiral, "and hear him before we judge him."

So a Quaker meeting was arranged at Macroom
Castle. All the Penns were there and their servants; a
few of the Admiral's tenants, led by curiosity, dropped
in; and out from Cork with the preacher came a little
group of Quakers. William recognized among them the
woman who kept a shop where they sometimes bought
supplies.

The Admiral kept his hat on in the house, of course; it
was a chilly day, and it was his house. Equally of course
William and the tutor did not wear theirs in his presence,
and the neighbors who came in respectfully uncovered.
But the Quakers wore theirs. Though they were but
shopkeepers and carpenters and small farmers and the
Admiral was a gentleman and the owner of a great estate, still these plain people kept their hats on. William
watched with wide-open eyes to see what his father
would do, but though he frowned, he said nothing.

The company settled down on chairs and benches in
the great hall of the castle. The Quakers, or Friends of
the Truth as they called themselves, sat with their hands
folded in their laps and looked down. Their faces were
quiet and peaceful and strangely happy. The church
people looked self-conscious and restless, as if they were
wondering what their friends would think if they could
see them now, and when something would happen. William looked at Thomas Loe to see if he was going to
quake, but he sat there with his arms folded.

Gradually, he hardly knew when or how, William felt the silence stealing through him, like a tide coming in, a silence that seemed to be full of meaning. He remembered that day in his room in Chigwell and how he had felt then.

Thomas Loe rose and began to speak. For all his frieze coat and plain hat, he was an educated man and his speech was clear and powerful. Everybody in the room was listening. He said that men did not need priests to speak to God for them, that God was the inward light in every man's own soul. He said much more that William did not understand or even hear, for he was watching the faces of those who were listening. Their every-day masks had melted and their deepest feelings moved in their defenseless faces.

William heard a great gulp and a sob behind him, and realized that the black boy Jack was crying. He looked at his father; tears stood in the Admiral's eyes.

Stricken by the sight of something he had never imagined could be, William said to himself with a gone feeling in his heart: "What if we should all become Quakers!"

But they didn't. After a day or two Thomas Loe went on foot to Dublin to preach there, and life at Macroom Castle settled back into its regular ways. The Admiral said that he agreed with the Quakers about not swearing. "Swear not at all . . . let your communication be, Yea, yea; Nay, nay," the Bible said plainly—and he had refused oaths himself on his expedition to the West Indies. But the Quakers were a simple folk; there were few educated men among them. Their thee-ing and thou-ing, their refusal of hat-honor, and their attitude toward war made their way of life inconvenient for people who had a position in the world to keep up. Before long, only William remembered that living silence and the tears in his father's eyes.

The years in that lovely, lonely, moist, green land slipped past. William studied with his tutor, he roamed over his father's farms and woods, he ran and rode horseback. He grew tall and slim and hard-muscled, he learned all his father had time to teach him about managing an estate, he carried himself well when he met the Admiral's friends—and he had no idea how proud his father was of him.

Oliver Cromwell died and his son Richard took his place, Richard who was so weak and uncertain that soon people were calling him Tumbledown Dick. The army became the real ruler, and army rule is never anything but arbitrary and unjust.

All over the country people began to remember that they had a king in Holland. First a voice here and there, then a general murmur that became a thunder of command called for a new Parliament to meet and bring the King back. Admiral Penn went to London. In April 1660 he was chosen to represent the nautical borough of Weymouth in the new Parliament. In May he was sent with ships to King Charles II to bid him welcome home to England.

On the twenty-third of May, he was knighted by the King on the *Naseby*, which was henceforth to be called the *Royal Charles*, and made a commissioner of the Navy, with a salary of five hundred pounds and a house in the Navy Gardens in London.

The King had come into his own again—as the popular ballad had it—and so had Sir William Penn.

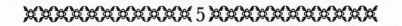

5

Gentleman Commoner

THAT October the family that had for four years lived
so affectionate and self-contained a life on their
estate at distant Macroom was scattered. Lady Penn and
the two younger children remained in Ireland; Sir
William Penn, Navy Commissioner, was in London;
Son William went to Oxford. He was entered as a
gentleman commoner at Christ Church, one of the most
aristocratic colleges in that highly aristocratic seat of
learning. The knight's son was sent to mingle with the
sons of dukes and earls and get an education that would
fit him to be an ambassador or a statesman.

Young William Penn was sixteen. Oxford was a mad
and exciting place to be that year of the Restoration. All
through the time of the Commonwealth and Oliver
Cromwell's rule, Oxford had remained secretly loyal to
the exiled King, and now that Charles II had been re-
stored to the throne of England, all Oxford went crazy
with joy. Everything that belonged to the Commonwealth or smacked of Puritanism they flung aside. They
threw out Dr. John Owen, the broad-minded Puritan
who had been dean of Christ Church and vice-chancellor
of the university, and put a churchman in his place. For

the sober Puritan virtues the scholars had even less use. They went laughing and shouting and swearing and drinking healths to King Charles II in the streets. They wore the most extravagant clothes, coats of silk and satin and velvet, embroidered waistcoats, lace cravats, breeches with deep lace frills at the knee and ribbon rosettes, shoes with silver buckles. They wore long curly wigs—very convenient for covering your cropped head if you had been a Puritan once and wanted people to forget it now—they carried swords, and muffs too when the weather was cold. Their time as well as their money they spent on drinking, dancing, cards, and riotous parties. Nobody thought of studying. Anybody who studied was a "fanatic." Anybody who so much as breathed the word "moderation" was a "rebel."

Into all this came Son William, fresh from his lonely Irish castle and his strict upbringing. He took his place, however, without any trouble. He too had a curly wig and a sword; he had moreover a lively and sweet-tempered disposition, a quick wit, a strong and active body. He could do anything that he set his mind to. When it became fashionable to write elegies on the death of the Duke of Gloucester, the King's younger brother, William wrote a poem in Latin, and very good it was too, elegant and loyal, and sound Latin to boot. And when he went in for athletics—"manly sports," they called them—there too he quickly made a name for himself. Foot-racing (the favorite sport of his Chigwell days), jumping, riding, and sword-play—he was good at all of them.

He had, however, something else besides; he had a brilliant and eager mind, and he could not help using it. He studied Latin and Greek, rhetoric, some logic, which he did not like, for he thought it was taught in a pedantic way, and some theology, which was a popular subject even at Oxford. Every well-educated man could argue on fine points of doctrine even though he might not have the slightest desire to put any of it into practice. He went to the anatomy lecture which was given every spring after the Lent assizes. The body of a criminal who had been at that time conveniently condemned and hanged was dissected by a chirurgeon before the students, while the King's professor of physic held forth on the human anatomy. There he ran across John Locke, a young don still in his twenties, and they listened together to the lecture, unaware of the ways they were to know each other later on.

In April his father sent for him to come up to London to see the coronation of King Charles II. It was a two days' journey from Oxford to London, and he spent the night on the way at Penn in Bucks, where some distant relatives of his had a manor house. It was the first time he had seen Buckinghamshire when the primroses were out and the birds beginning to sing in the beech woods.

As he got nearer to London, he found the highroad full of people going to the coronation. London itself was crowded, and gay with decorations: banners and flowers and bright carpets that hung from windows and balconies. For days workmen had been building triumphal arches along the path of the procession, and everyone was thinking about the weather and hoping for the best.

His father's house was on the north side of the Navy Gardens in Seething Lane, a most convenient location, for it was near the Navy Office where he spent the better part of his days, and near the river too. It was within sight of the Tower of London; and All Hallows Church, where William had been baptized, was just at the end of the lane. The Navy commissioners, however, all went to St. Olav's Church in Hart Street, where a special pew had been built for them in the gallery. Another house in the Navy Gardens belonged to Sir William Batten, their old friend at Walthamstow, who was now a Navy Commissioner also; and a Mr. Samuel Pepys, who was Clerk of the Acts, lived in still another. He seemed a lively, inquisitive little man with bright black eyes and full cheeks, very fond of music and of having a finger in every pie. A hard worker, too, Sir William said. The houses were all alike, in a row, and all had been freshly done over by their new inhabitants. There was a garden common to all with tiled terraces where the householders enjoyed walking and talking together. Sometimes Mr. Pepys brought out his flageolet or his violin and played for them. The Penns' house inside looked a bit bare and forlorn, as houses do when men are keeping bachelor's hall in them, but Mr. and Mrs. Pepys had theirs in fine style, with green serge and gilt leather in the dining-room and some very fine pictures and maps.

The coronation ceremony itself was to take place in Westminster Abbey on April 23, but an even greater spectacle was the coronation procession the day before, from the Tower to Whitehall Palace.

The Penns had a fine place from which to see it. They, with Sir William Batten and his family, and the Pepyses, had arranged to rent a room with windows on the line of march in a flagmaker's house in Cornhill, right near the naval arch, which was very handsome indeed, being painted with gods and goddesses and Kings Charles I and II.

They were there early, for the streets would soon be so crowded that people could not push through, but they did not find the waiting tiresome. They had the room all to themselves, and they were a congenial group. So they passed the time with wine and cake and talk and laughter. Mr. Pepys in his new velvet coat made them all very merry by winking at some pretty ladies in a window across the street.

William found other things to see in the street outside: the common people gathering and lustily cheering the men who came in carts to throw gravel over the muddy street, the London militia arriving to line the way six feet or so apart, and at last, after several hours, the sound of trumpets, and the cavalcade itself.

The Horse Guards came first; then the sixty-eight Knights of the Bath in their crimson robes; then the bishops in full ecclesiastical panoply, and the barons, earls, marquises, and their heralds, all in such a splendor of gold and silver and diamonds that the spring sun on it all but blinded you. The Lord Mayor of London passed. The crowd pressed forward, their cheers mounting; the Duke of York, the younger brother of the King, was coming.

Sir William Penn was tense, his hand on young William's shoulder. "The Duke!" he said. "Son William, he is only eleven years older than you are."

So young William Penn saw for the first time the man who was to be his friend: he came riding on a stiffly prancing horse, shining with gold and white and scarlet and jewels, with his magnificent wig spread out over his shoulders and his face between the lovelocks narrow and dark and serious.

When he saw the group in the flagmaker's window, he looked up and bowed, not as he bowed for the crowd, but specially. Mr. Pepys puffed and strutted like a pouter pigeon, but William knew it was for his father, that special notice. Had it not been Admiral Penn who was sent by the Parliament to welcome James and Charles Stuart back to England?

The Lord High Constable came next, and then the Earl Marshal, bearing the sword of state before the King in his coronation robes.

The shouting rose to frenzied shrillness. William looked down with awe at majesty passing so close beneath him, and the young King, who was not yet thirty, raised heavy-lidded eyes and flashed a smile in his turn toward the group in the window.

The King and the Duke of York both had noticed Sir William Penn!

My Lord Monk, who had been a general of the fleet with Sir William in the days of the Dutch War, rode behind the King, leading a spare horse. The procession dwindled away with a company of foot-soldiers, young and comely in white doublets, and a company of men dressed for some obscure reason like Turks. It was all over. Mr. Pepys said he was pleased beyond imagination at what he had seen.

Mr. Young the flagmaker brought dinner to the company in his parlor, and after eating it they all went home. That night the fountains in the city ran wine instead of water, there were speeches at the triumphal arches, music and dancing in the narrow streets, bonfires in the open places. William and Mr. Pepys's boy went to see a show on Tower Hill.

All evening long the bells rang; every church rang a special peal of bells, some of them lasting as long as three hours without stopping. It is strange to think that church bells should ring so joyously to usher in a time when men were to be persecuted cruelly for worshiping God according to their consciences, but so it was.

William went back to the university. Gradually, more and more, he became troubled by the life there.

The new dean of Christ Church brought back the old elaborate ritual of the days before the Commonwealth to the services in the college chapel. William, who well knew his fellow students and their riotous ways, now saw them in the distracting beauty of the chapel, wearing surplices and caps and bowing and singing and sanctimoniously reading responses out of a book—and going on their hilarious way out of church the same as ever. The insincerity of the whole performance disgusted him. He thought it would be better not to go to church at all than to go and mock religion thus.

Another boy who thought as he did introduced him to Dr. John Owen, who since his dismissal from Christ Church had been living in the suburbs of Oxford. He was a friend of Lord Broghill, the Penns' friend in Ireland, and so he was interested in William from the first, and William in him. He was a man who got on well with boys; he was passionately fond of playing the flute, which was fashionable at that time, he was a good athlete himself and interested in sports, he was fiery in defense of his principles, chief of which was religious liberty. Boys liked to go to his house to talk about the great problems of the day, religion and politics, and air their views, which could not be spoken aloud in college. In spite of the laws against all religious groups that were outside of the Established Church, Dr. Owen held services in his house for those boys who were determined to think for themselves.

For all his broadmindedness, however, Dr. Owen had no sympathy for the Quakers. There had been a few in Oxford within the last six years, but they had been punished by the authorities and maltreated by the students because of their fanatical ways of trying to startle people into listening to their teachings, and most of those who were left in the city were in prison.

William had sometimes an unhappy feeling that he had not found what he sought even at Dr. Owen's house, but still he was quite sure it was better than the college chapel, to which he stopped going altogether.

The authorities soon got wind of it. William and the rest of his group were fined.

His father was not long in hearing about it, and Son William was summoned forthwith to London. He went reluctantly, for he dreaded his father's displeasure. He had always been "tender under rebuke," and his mother, who was still in Ireland, could not intercede for him this time.

It was not after all so bad as he had expected. Sir William was annoyed; he didn't want his son to be queer and singular among his fellows at the university. It was a block in the way of preferment. He said so with emphasis. As to William's conscience, he snorted, he was only seventeen and he could leave that in the care of people older and wiser than he. Son William was to go back to college and conform to the rules like anybody else.

When that was over, William had rather a pleasant little vacation out of it. He had a whole day, while his father was at Westminster with Mr. Pepys, to roam the city by himself, to watch the boats coming and going on the river and speculate about a frigate in the Pool that was bound, so they said, for America. He remembered a vivid discussion he had had with some others at college

about some recent books setting forth ideal governments, and someone had said, why not start a Utopia in
the American colonies, where there was so much fresh
land that hadn't had a chance to be spoiled. William's
mind had opened joyfully to the idea of a perfect government with religious liberty for everyone. He remembered
that talk when he looked at the boat being loaded for
America.

That evening after his father and Mr. Pepys came
home, they sent for him to go over to Mr. Pepys's
house, where they supped and talked and made merry till
late.

Pegg was in London now, too, at a boarding school in
Clerkenwell. When Christmas came, both she and
William had holidays, and they had great times in Navy
Gardens. Mrs. Pepys was keeping an eye on Pegg, since
her mother was not there to do it, and as a result they
saw a good deal of the Pepyses during those days.

The day after Christmas they all went by coach to
Moorfields to walk, but it was so cold and sleety that
they had to go into an ale house to warm up with cakes
and ale. That night the three Penns supped with the
Pepyses on turkey and were very merry over a game of
cards afterwards. Pegg was wearing a flowered satin
suit that Mrs. Pepys had helped her to get, and William
thought she was not a bad-looking little thing at all,
though entirely too forward for a ten-year-old.

On New Year's Day the Pepyses took Pegg and
William to the Duke's Theatre to see the *Spanish Cu-*

rate. Everybody went to plays now, and it was strange to think that only a short time ago they were not permitted by law! Afterward, when they were back at the Pepyses' house playing cards, William suddenly had a terrible sense of loss and clapped his hand to his side. He had! He had left his sword in the coach! He threw down his cards and was up at once to go hunt for it. Mr. Pepys laughed uproariously and said it was like looking for a needle in a haystack, but out William rushed, with Mr. Pepys's boy after him. Down Hart Street they went, and up Mark Lane to Leadenhall Street, scrutinizing every coach they passed, down Leadenhall Street to Cornhill, and there at the Exchange they met with the very same coach they had ridden in, hatchet-faced coachman and all. William flung open the door. His sword was inside, just where he had left it. He was unspeakably relieved, and Mr. Pepys, when they got back, laughed louder than ever.

The sixth of January they celebrated the Penns' wedding anniversary as they always did, with a chine of beef and other good things, and a great dish of mince pies—eighteen this time, one for each year. The Battens and the Pepyses, Colonel Treswell and Major Holmes were the guests, and everyone was sorry that Lady Penn was still in Ireland. On the eighth Pegg went back to school in Clerkenwell, and William to Oxford.

Oxford in winter was damp and cold and gray. The Christ Church Meadows were wet, with a thin film of ice on the mud. The great hall of the college was dim and chill in spite of the fire that smoldered on the hearth and occasionally flared up to stir the shadows among the great Irish oak beams of the roof or strike colors out of the stained glass windows. The stone chapel with its pillars and carved round arches had a death-like iciness, and when the scholars in their surplices sang their *Te Deums*, their breath rose in white feathers in the grayness.

It was a time for setting one's teeth and going ahead with what one had to do, no matter what other people said. William's decision to follow his conscience was not made in the top of his mind; it happened somewhere in the depths of his being, like a river slowly pushing through a dam. In spite of the deans and the dons, in spite of the fines, in spite of his father, he went no more to the college chapel but rode out to Dr. Owen's house instead, and when he could not go there, he held meetings in his own rooms.

In March he was expelled.

He had nowhere else to go but to London, to his father.

Sir William Penn had been an admiral; he was accustomed to command not only ships but whole squadrons, and to regard disobedience as mutiny. William had disobeyed him. He had disappointed him. Here was his brilliant and handsome son, well placed in the world, who could go far if only he kept his head, and what did he do? Ruined his chances. Sir William was exasperated almost beyond endurance, for he had had sympathy for the boy; he had been dissatisfied with Oxford and had consulted Mr. Pepys about Magdalene College, Cambridge, and was even now waiting to hear about a Mr. Burton who was a tutor there. If only William had waited, he might have left Christ Church honorably.

He told William in bitter and stinging words what he thought of his folly, and then growing angrier the longer he thought about it, he finished by thrashing him.

Walking in the garden later with Mr. Pepys, Sir William told his inquisitive neighbor that Son William was at home "not well," which was true enough.

Still later, thrashing not having improved William's undesirable state of mind, he turned him out of doors.

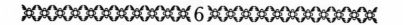

6

The Grand Tour

THEY were not long estranged, those two who so deeply loved and admired—and hurt—each other. Son William was soon home again, and the Admiral was busy seeking another and a better way than blows to rid the boy of his unfortunate ideas. Perhaps his friend, the Duke of Ormonde, lately made viceroy of Ireland, helped him to find it. At any rate, by midsummer he had it. The "grand tour," of course! William, like most of the fashionable youths since the days of Queen Elizabeth, should finish his education with a grand tour of France, Switzerland, and Italy. He had had too quiet a life there in Ireland with his tutor, and then at Oxford that Dr. Owen had got him under his influence. Now let him go out and see the world!

He could not go alone, of course. Other "persons of quality" must be found to accompany him. By great good luck the Scottish Earl of Crawford was taking his son and some young companions to Paris, and it was arranged that William should start off with them.

On the fifth of July he and his father went to the Pepyses' house for a farewell dinner, and by the middle of the month both were out of London, the Admiral off to Ireland with the Duke of Ormonde and a great retinue, and William to Dover, Calais, and Paris! The house in Navy Gardens was shut up, and poor Pegg, stuck in her school in Clerkenwell, must have felt forlorn indeed.

Travelers making the grand tour went by boat from London to Gravesend, where they took post to Dover. From Dover they went by packet-boat to Calais and thence in six days by coach to Paris. Wherever else they were going, they went to Paris first, for Paris was the most brilliant and glittering city in Europe and set the styles for all the civilized world.

Grand tourists in Paris did three things. As soon as they got there, they rushed forth and ordered French clothes. Then while these were being made, they went sightseeing in their old clothes, to see the Pont Neuf with the copper statue of Henry the Great on horseback, the Louvre, Notre Dame, the University (which English visitors never thought quite so fine as Oxford), the Sorbonne, which had been made over by Richelieu into a magnificent modern building, and the gardens of the Tuileries, where they walked under the famous elms and mulberry trees. Meanwhile they had presented all the letters of introduction to French notables that they had been able to scrape up, and when their new clothes were ready, they went out into society.

The Earl of Crawford and his party were received at the court of Louis XIV, that dazzling "young Apollo" who was known as *le roi soleil*. Young William Penn, who was barely eighteen, and at that not so very much

"The gentleman . . . unsheathed his sword and went for William"

younger than King Louis, learned court manners by watching the rest, and no doubt in moments when he felt overwhelmed by all the grandeur was strengthened by the memory of King Charles II of England on his way to his coronation taking notice of Sir William Penn in the flag-maker's window. But London and London's King seemed homely and informal compared with Paris and its court.

In Paris too he met the Countess of Sunderland, who had been Lady Dorothy Sidney, the grand-niece of the great Sir Philip. She had been a beauty in her day and a famous poet had written verses to her calling her Sach-

arissa; now she was old enough to have a son, Robert
Spencer, who was four years older than William—and
quite the most engaging and knowledgeable young man
William had ever met. A friendship sprang up between
them that was to last for years.

One night during his stay in Paris, William, attended
by the Earl of Crawford's servant, was going back to his
lodgings at about eleven o'clock after some party or
other. The Paris streets were dark and muddy and none
too savory, and he was hurrying along so intently that
he failed to see that a gentleman who passed him had
taken off his hat to him. He pressed on without returning
the salute. The gentleman, insulted, promptly and furiously unsheathed his sword and went for William.

Not for nothing had William excelled in manly sports
at Oxford. Surprised by the suddenness of the attack and
amazed at the excitability of these Frenchmen, he drew
his own sword just in time. Catching his balance, he
parried several thrusts, and then, with swift skill, delivered an attack that sent his opponent's sword flying
out of his hand to bring up with a ringing clatter against
the stone wall behind him. The Frenchman, his flush of
anger fading into pallor in the flaring light of the torches
which the servants carried, was left standing there, dis-
armed, without even the dignity of a wound. William
sheathed his sword, swept off his hat with a flourish, explained his previous omission, and went on again, followed by the Earl of Crawford's reverentially admiring
servant. It takes real skill to disarm an opponent without

nicking him, and in a narrow street, at night, by torchlight.

Pleased with himself, at the moment, William could not help being, but later it struck him as a shock that one or the other of them might so easily have been killed. As if the ceremony of taking off a hat were worth a man's life!

Late that autumn he parted from the Earl of Crawford and went to Saumur, in Anjou, where he stayed for more than a year studying at the Huguenot Academy there. He liked the little city on the banks of the Loire, which had been a Roman camp and a medieval stronghold and now, in spite of its ancient tower and castle, was a thriving modern town with a theater and a museum and a large library, and a variety of manufactories, ranging from enamel and glassware to white wine.

Dr. Moses Amyraut was the head of the college, and William soon gave him his complete liking and respect. He reminded him a little of Dr. John Owen, especially in his enthusiasm for religious liberty, but he was a broader, wiser, more mellow person, and very scholarly. Someone had written an epigram about him that every new student heard quoted so often, when he first came, that he never forgot it.

> *"From Moses down to Moses, none*
> *Among the sons of men*
> *With equal luster ever shone*
> *In manners, tongue, and pen."*

Which was very nice, though possibly a trifle excessive.

Saumur was different from Oxford. The boys worked here. They read the Greek and Latin classics, attended lectures on theology given in French, and studied thoroughly the language, literature, and history of France. There was another difference: here were no religious controversies. Protestants of all kinds studied side by side with Roman Catholics.

In 1664 the great Dr. Amyraut died, and William, finding Saumur suddenly empty and flat, packed up ánd went on with his grand tour. He picked up Robert Spencer again, who had come back to France because his parents were determined to marry him to Lady Ann Digby and he had no idea of being thus disposed of without being properly consulted.

So the two boys in the highest spirits went traveling through Switzerland to Italy. William looked up to Robert; he was so gay, so fascinating, he knew his way about Europe as William might know the neighborhood of the Navy Office, he made friends wherever he went, not because he was the future Earl of Sunderland but because he was such extraordinarily good company. If he had some darker and less desirable traits of character, William did not see them. He was like that always; if he liked people, he saw no flaws in them. It was a quality that made him a good friend but a poor judge of men, and it got him often into trouble.

It was probably in Turin that they met Spencer's republican uncle, Algernon Sidney, who was in exile for his opposition to King Charles II. He had very little money to live on, and much time to read and think, and what he thought about was government and liberty. He was as old as William's father, but William always got on well with older men. He liked Algernon Sidney at once, and he took fire with the thought of liberty in government as he had flamed to Dr. Owen's and Dr. Amyraut's passion for liberty in religion. It was only a brief meeting, but they both remembered it, and years later when William Penn wanted to make out a plan for a government that was to be really free, it was Algernon Sidney whom he got to help him with it.

Turin, their first city in Italy, was dull. They were preparing to press on to Rome, to Florence, to Venice, when a message came from Sir William Penn. England was on the eve of war with the Dutch; France, the ancient enemy, showed signs of joining the Hollanders; Sir William was going back into the Navy as commander of a squadron. Son William was to come home at once to take his place as head of the household in his father's absence.

It was lucky that Son William was so good a horseman. He rode post-haste across France and was back in London in mid-August. He was proud to be called on to play a man's part—and he was truly glad to see his family again.

His mother, who had just come from Ireland, he had not seen for four years, his father for two. Pegg at thirteen was grown a fine lady; little Dickie was eight years old, "a notable, stout, witty boy," as their ever-present friend Mr. Pepys said. They were all bathed in happiness, for they were a very affectionate family indeed, and they had so much to tell and to hear.

The Admiral especially was beaming with pride and joy—and more than a touch of self-congratulation. How wise he had been! Here was Son William as he had always hoped to see him: handsome, courtly in his manners, modish in appearance—though the Admiral did not care much for those new French pantaloon breeches; he could sing French songs and talk amusingly about French ways, he was learned without a trace of vanity. And above all he had forgotten those wild unmodish notions of religion that had once threatened to be troublesome.

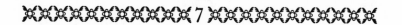

7

Dispatches for the King

Now and for nearly a year to come the Penns were happy together, in spite of the shadow of war that hung over them. The Admiral was busy with the work he was best fitted for—organizing the Navy, which had fallen into sad disrepair; and Lady Penn was delighted to have her family all under one roof once more. They were more intimate than ever with their neighbors, the Pepyses. Scarcely a week passed that they were not at one house or the other for supper or games or cards. Dickie was Mrs. Pepys's valentine; Mr. Pepys admired Pegg's new colored silk suit with the silver lace; Pegg and Mrs. Pepys took drawing lessons from the same master—and it went hard with Pegg that Mrs. Pepys achieved the better pictures. The Pepyses came in to look at and exclaim over Lady Penn's glass bowl in which some rare little foreign yellow fish swam about in water as happily as if it had been the sea, and the Penns went to dine on roast swan at the Pepyses' house. William was his father's close companion until in February he began to study law at Lincoln's Inn.

Lincoln's Inn was one of the four great Inns of Court where young men studied to be barristers. It was situated

on Chancery Lane, and to get there William walked
every day through the city past St. Paul's and its churchyard where the booksellers' shops were full of prints and
maps as well as books, down Ludgate Street, past the
entrance to the Old Bailey, where the Sessions House and
Newgate Prison were, and down the length of Fleet
Street to the Temple and Chancery Lane. He was glad
when he reached Lincoln's Inn, for after the narrow,
crowded, ill-smelling streets of the city, which the upper
stories of houses overhung so far that apprentices could
lean out of attic windows and shake hands across the
street, Lincoln's Inn seemed very fresh and open, almost
like the country. Lincoln's Inn Fields, with its grass and
trees and paths, was a favorite place for people to go
walking on Sunday afternoons.

All that autumn and winter the Admiral worked to
prepare the fleet for war. New ships were needed, and
repairs for the old ones. The Admiral had to get timber,
iron, hemp, gun-wads, mast-yards, and other neces-
saries; he had to have men, too, not only seamen but
carpenters, shipwrights, smiths, joiners, calkers, sawyers;
he had to lay in great stores of provisions—and for all
this he needed money. Parliament had, it is true, granted
a huge sum of money for the purpose, but the King, that
merry monarch who took nothing very seriously, was
squandering a good part of it on his own personal pleasures and extravagances at court. It was altogether a busy
and nerve-racking time for the Admiral, and he, having
suffered from gout ever since his sojourn in the Tower

ten years before, found it heavy going. But when war was finally declared, early in March 1665, the fleet was almost ready.

The Duke of York was Lord High Admiral of the English Navy. He was an earnest young man, but he knew nothing of the sea or of naval warfare, and so Admiral Penn was given the title of Great Captain Commander and put on the Duke's flagship, the *Royal Charles*, to tell him what to do. That would have been easy enough, but he had a flock of younger officers besides who knew even less and had no earnestness at all, young courtiers like the Earl of Falmouth and Lord Muskerry, who went to sea because it was suddenly a fashionable thing to do and seemed to promise much excitement and fame for little effort. They were an exasperating lot—all but one. That one was the Great Captain Commander's own son, young William Penn.

William had a month at sea in close companionship with his father and the Duke of York. It was on the whole a very tiresome month. Nothing happened. A few Dutch scouts came out and were chased. The fleet could not issue forth to challenge the enemy because they had to wait for provisions to arrive, and the longer they were delayed the hungrier and more restless the sailors became. The young courtiers of the *Royal Charles* were sadly bored; they quarreled among themselves and took offense at Admiral Penn, who they thought should have respected their rank, even though he obviously could not respect their seamanship.

At last, toward the end of April, the fleet of a hundred and three ships was ready for an engagement. Tenseness swept through the crews. The Lord High Admiral and the Great Captain Commander, having dispatches to send to the King, picked out young William Penn to carry them. His month at sea was over.

He departed unwillingly, for it is hard to leave just when things are going to begin, and no doubt it was whispered among the young courtiers that the Admiral was whisking his son out of danger; but orders were orders, and it was something to be the bearer of important messages to the King.

Sir William Coventry, the Duke's secretary, wrote on April 22 to the Secretary of State: "Mr. Penn will relate our condition under sail with a brave fleet, wind and weather fair." Mr. Penn, however, was not much of a sailor, and after his passage in a small boat from the *Royal Charles* off Orfordness to the town of Harwich some forty or fifty miles away, he considered the weather by no means fair.

He landed at Harwich about noon on Sunday, and having some time to wait before he could get a horse, he wrote a note to his father and sent it back by the boat that had brought him there.

"From Harwich, 23rd April 1665.
"Honored Father:
"We could not arrive here sooner than this day, about twelve of the clock, by reason of the continued cross winds

and, as I thought, foul weather. I pray God, after all the foul weather and dangers you are exposed to, and shall be, that you come home as secure. And I bless God my heart does not in any way fail, but firmly believe that if God has called you out to battle, he will cover your head in that smoky day. And as I never knew what a father was till I had wisdom enough to prize him, so I can safely say that now of all times your concerns are most dear to me. It's hard, meantime, to lose both a father and a friend.

"W.P."

He took post at three o'clock of that same day, which was the swiftest possible way to cover the seventy miles between Harwich and London. Even so he had to travel all night long. Before daylight had quite come he was hurrying through Stratford-Bow, and by Aldgate into the city. To his left the Tower of London lifted its four turrets into the dawn-filled sky, and he knew that almost within its shadow people in the Navy Gardens were beginning to stretch and stir, that possibly his mother, anxious about her two Williams, was watching the morning come through her casement. But he could not stop; he had messages for the King.

Through the early streets he posted, scattering sleepy apprentices who were out early and sleepy roisterers who were out late. Down Leadenhall Street, down Cornhill, where the flagmaker's shop was shuttered and sleeping, down Cheapside, past St. Paul's, down Fleet Street and the Strand, past Charing Cross, and down the last stretch to the palace of Whitehall, which sat solidly on the bank of the Thames with the tower of St. Margaret's Church and the roofs of the Abbey looming up beyond it.

William knew his way about the palace. The long stone gallery upstairs, with the paintings by Rubens and Correggio and Van Dyck, was the place where you waited for an audience with the King.

His Majesty was not yet up. William presented himself to Lord Arlington, the Secretary of State, and Colonel Ashburnham, the King's bodyguard. He had scarcely begun to tell them his errand when the King in the next room, hearing voices, set up a great knocking to know what was going on. Colonel Ashburnham hastened to tell him that there was an express from the Duke of York. At which, "earnestly skipping out of bed," as William described it to his father later, His Majesty the King of England came bounding forth clad only in his dressing-gown and slippers. When he saw William, he said: "Oh, is't you? How is Sir William?"

For more than half an hour they talked thus informally, King Charles in his gown and William in his rumpled traveling clothes, the King asking questions—asking three different times how Sir William Penn was—and William answering and delivering all the messages and letters. At length the King said:

"Go now about Sir William's business—and your own too," and William was free to take the news to his mother.

Not till the third of June did the battle come off. Then

it was fought off Lowestoft about a hundred and twenty miles away to the northeast, and though the guns were heard at Dover, they did not carry to London. It was another great battle for the English fleet, and for Admiral Penn, who all day long from three in the morning till ten at night, clad in a full suit of armor and suffering agonies from the gout, directed the fighting and the maneuvers.

The news of the victory reached London a few days later, and great was the rejoicing in the Penn household in the Navy Gardens. Mr. Pepys came in to congratulate them, and then they all went together to a neighbor's great room, and after that down into the street where they built a great bonfire at the gate. All over the city joy flamed up in the clear late twilight, and young William Penn's pride in his father glowed too, like a flame. As Mr. Pepys said, they were all "not a little puffed up," but even he—and William could not help noticing that their vivacious neighbor was at times gnawed by the tooth of jealousy—admitted that good service had been done by the Admiral.

Underneath the joy and the triumph, however, a deep uneasiness and foreboding began to be felt. The plague! For more than a year they had been hearing about it at intervals: it was in Amsterdam; it was rumored in London in December; in April two or three houses had been shut up. People talked of remedies, some saying one thing, some another. Mr. Pepys thought that if you chewed tobacco it kept off infection—but everyone knew in his heart that few who caught it ever recovered. The very day before the news of the battle had come, Mr. Pepys had seen some houses in Drury Lane marked with a red cross on the door and the words scrawled in red chalk: "Lord have mercy on us all."

During that June of hot sultry days and nights lit by heat lightning, the plague swept down upon the defenseless city. Terror was written on every blanched face. It came so fast, so relentlessly. In June, it took two hundred and sixty-five people. The second week in July, eleven hundred died; the third, two thousand. The first week in August the number of deaths reached four thousand. By September eight thousand were dying weekly. Coffins were piled up in the streets, and at night a cart went by with a man ringing a bell and calling somberly: "Bring out your dead!"

At first the streets were full of people fleeing from town in coaches and wagons and carts; then suddenly they were empty, so that you could walk all morning and meet with only two coaches and a cart or so the whole way, and almost as few people on foot. Grass sprang up in the muddy streets and flourished, for there were not enough footsteps to trample it down. There is no more ominous sight than grass growing in the streets of a great city.

The King and his courtiers left Whitehall and went to Hampton Court, up the Thames. The Parliament went to Oxford. The clergy with one accord abandoned their churches and their parishioners and rushed to the country to save themselves. Mr. Pepys sent his wife to

Woolwich early in July, but he stayed on in London himself to attend to the Navy Office business. Admiral Penn was still away with the fleet, but the rest of his family were in the Navy Gardens.

William went doggedly on with his law studies at Lincoln's Inn and found in Coke's *Institutes*—that great work on the common law—an escape from the vast problems of life and death that everyone who lived through those days had to think about. The few people who were seen in the streets carried the possibility of death in their faces, and when two stopped to talk with one another, they spoke as if they two might not meet again. Even the lighthearted Mr. Pepys was "setting things in order, both as to soul and body."

Though Dr. Mills, the rector of St. Olav's, had left his congregation to meet sickness and death and sorrow without spiritual help from him, the bell-ringers and the grave-diggers stayed at their post. All day long in the Navy Gardens they could hear the "surly solemn bell" tolling for deaths or burials, and when Lady Penn and Pegg went to church, they had to pick their way among the mounds of new graves that were heaped up one on top of another in the little churchyard.

When the pulpits of the Established Church were left empty by their rectors, the Non-Conformist preachers and ministers stepped in and preached from them. Quakers were holding their meetings openly and going about from house to house, and to the prisons too, visiting the sick and poor. Some people called them "the angels of the plague." Others said that the plague was a judgment on them for their blasphemous beliefs.

Meanwhile the court, safe in the pure country air, went on its frivolous and uncaring way, as extravagantly dressed as ever, as busy with cards and music and love-affairs; and the Parliament, safe in Oxford, passed laws with more severe penalties than ever against all those who differed from the Established Church. They did it, they said, to protect their religion.

Young William Penn, who would be twenty-one in October, heard of these things, and was weighed down with a sense of "the vanity of this world, and the ir-religiousness of the religions of it."

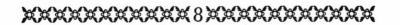

8

A Young Man of Affairs

WHEN a young man's head and heart are in a turmoil over wrongs too vast and complicated for him to set right, his elders, if they are wise, find him some hard work to do. The Admiral, who came home in the late autumn and recognized at once the signs of perturbation in his son, speedily found a job for William, and one that would take him clean out of London too.

Accordingly, soon after Christmas William set forth once more, with his fine Paris clothes and the sumpter horse that had carried his luggage in France, to put his newly acquired legal knowledge to practical use in Ireland. He had letters of introduction to the Duke of Ormonde in Dublin, and he had his father's new estate of Shangarry to take care of. He was no longer a student, he was a man of twenty-one with important affairs in hand, which his father, who was busy getting England's battered Navy in condition to fight some more, could not attend to himself. He felt happier already.

He sailed up the harbor of Kinsale past the great bluff called the Old Head of Kinsale, and landed at the fort of which his father was now, though absent, officially the governor—and captain, too, of the company of foot-

63

soldiers stationed there. Instead of going on to Macroom, twenty-four miles west of Cork in the hills,
William turned eastward to Shangarry.

It was a lovely place. The Celtic name meant the Old
Garden, and a garden it was, with its eight square miles
of lush green fields almost surrounded by water. On the
east was a broad estuary, on the south the ocean, on the
west beautiful Cork Harbor. The old castle, which had
once held out against Queen Elizabeth's troops, was now
in ruins, having been destroyed by Cromwell's order
nearly twenty years before, but two miles west of it there
was a pleasant old dwelling house called Sunville, where
William stayed. A number of small farms belonging to
the estate were rented out to English people; one of
these, William's Uncle George Penn had; and his son,
also William Penn, was clerk of the cheque at Kinsale.
There was, too, a modern house at Imokilly—but a
certain Colonel Wallis was living there.

William's business in Ireland was to get this same
Colonel Wallis removed from his father's estate. When
King Charles II came to the throne in 1660, there was a
general re-arranging of estates. The Earl of Clancarty,
who had been King Charles's friend, wanted to get back
his estate of Macroom, which Cromwell had taken away
from him to give to Admiral Penn. The King accordingly
took Macroom away from the Penns and returned it to
his lordship, and then, since the Admiral was also a
friend of his, he set about finding something for him
that would do as well or a little better. The place he

pitched on was Shangarry, which Cromwell had given to
Colonel Wallis, an officer in his army. The King put
Colonel Wallis out with no compunction, but Admiral
Penn kindly allowed him to stay on as a tenant until he

was ready to use the estate himself. Now, when because of his increasingly bad health he was thinking seriously about retiring one day to Ireland to live, he wanted to get Shangarry in order, and he asked Colonel Wallis to remove himself. That gentleman, however, maintained that Shangarry belonged to him; he said he had spent a great deal of money on it, putting in ditches to drain the fields and so forth; and furthermore he was there and there he was going to stay. The King's commissioners on the settlement of Ireland wrote and told him to get out, but possession, since time immemorial, had been nine points of the law, and Colonel Wallis sat tight. This was the legal tangle that young William Penn was sent to unravel.

At first everything went easily; he had a talk with the Colonel and they seemed to reach an agreement satisfactory to both. William wrote to his father about it on the twenty-sixth of January, and went to Dublin.

He presented himself forthwith at the vast and ancient Castle, where the Duke of Ormonde, who stood for the King in Ireland, had gathered all the most brilliant men in the country about him in state apartments that were shabby to the point of dilapidation. But if the rooms where court was held left something to be desired, the courtiers were glittering folk indeed. Lord Broghill, who was now the Earl of Orrery, came to Dublin frequently from his estate in Munster, and his younger brother, Lord Shannon, too. The Duke of Ormonde's two sons were there, Thomas, Lord Ossory, and Richard, Lord Arran.

Lord Arran, who was only eight years older than William, became almost immediately his friend and his idol. Both had been in France and loved it, both loved books, both were excellent athletes. William, who had immense capacities for hero-worship, admired his new friend with his whole heart, and for a time it seemed to him that young Lord Arran, who managed to be a courtier and a soldier and a man of understanding too, was just exactly what he would like to be himself.

That spring William followed his new friend into an adventure that might have changed the whole course of his life.

The garrison stationed at Carrickfergus, about ninety miles north of Dublin on the shore of Belfast Lough, suddenly rose against the King and seized the castle and the town. The news swept through Dublin and stirred the Lord Lieutenant to instant action. English domination of Ireland had never yet been final and complete, and the smallest revolt was something to be stamped out like a spark in a dry forest. The Lord Lieutenant sent his son, Lord Arran, with four companies of the regiment, to take Carrickfergus. William wasted no time debating; he volunteered at once, and went on the expedition as captain of one company.

Carrickfergus was a little sea-coast town of slate-roofed stone houses with a stout wall around it, defended by a castle with a great stone keep that mounted solidly on a jutting rock almost surrounded, at high tide, by water. It was not an easy place to storm, even with four companies, and the mutineers were desperate. It was no play battle for gentlemen's sons; there were sharp fighting and real danger that called for stout hearts and cool heads. A frigate in the royal navy, the *Dartmouth*, was sent by the Duke of Ormonde to stand by in Belfast Lough in case it should be needed, but it was not. Lord Arran and young William Penn—and the four companies, of course—did everything that was required.

When the day was over and the conquerors were in the castle keep, in the great hall called Fergus's Dining-Room, cooling their dry throats that stung with gunsmoke with delicious cold water from the famous well in the tower, William, in a burst of exaltation and triumph, decided that a soldier's life was the life for him.

Others thought so too. He had shown marked courage and coolness in the battle; Lord Arran spread the word, and he was praised on all sides. The Duke of Ormonde suggested that if Sir William were willing to give up his captaincy of the company of Kinsale, young William might very well take it over, and he wrote to the Admiral about it immediately. The captain of the *Dartmouth*, who happened to be William's cousin, Richard Rooth, also wrote to the Admiral about the mutiny, finishing by saying: "An account whereof I presume your honor have long since had from my cousin William, who was pleased to accompany his lordship in that action to his no small reputation." William wrote too—twice. He wanted very much to be captain of Kinsale.

The excitement—and the glory—had gone to his head as no wine ever could.

It was some time before he could hear from his father. While he was waiting, he went and had his portrait painted in his suit of armor, with his finest ruffles falling over his burnished steel chest, and his very best wig falling in waving locks over his burnished steel shoulders. Everyone who saw it praised the painting, and it showed indeed a handsome and spirited young man; but the face, as William even in his eagerness recognized deep down within him, was not the face of a soldier. The blue eyes were too thoughtful, the mouth too sensitive and kind.

Oddly enough, about the same time, Sir William was having his portrait painted by the fashionable Sir Peter Lely, at the command of the Duke of York, who wished to have all the famous captains who had been with him in his victory a year ago on the walls of his room. The Admiral did not wear his armor; he wore a velvet coat.

The Duke had written the Admiral on May 29, but he got no answer. Several times in the course of the month following he asked William about it, but though William had had a long and affectionate letter from his father, there had been in it not one word about the matter of the Kinsale company. Perhaps, he thought, the Duke's letter had never reached his father. He wrote again on the fourth of July: "I beseech your answer to this."

But the Admiral had had the letter; he had been thinking it over, thinking perhaps that the Kinsale command was profitable to him and that when he retired to Shangarry he might want it himself, thinking too that he had always intended to make an ambassador of Son William, not a soldier. At all events, ten days later he wrote:

"Son William:

"I have received two or three letters from you since I last wrote any to you. Besides my former advice I can say nothing but advise to sobriety and all those things that will speak you a Christian and a gentleman, which prudence may make to have the best consistency. As to the tender made by His Grace the Lord Lieutenant concerning the fort at Kinsale, I wish your youthful desires mayn't outrun your discretion. His Grace may, for a time, dispense with my absence— yours he will not, for so he told me. God bless, direct, and protect you.

"Your very affectionate father,
"W. Penn."

A baffling letter. William could not tell exactly what the Admiral was getting at in all that about dispensing with absences, and it was most annoying to one who was taking a man's part in the world to be admonished for youthful desires that outran discretion. What was perfectly clear, however, was the fact that Sir William was not going to give up the company at Kinsale to his son.

So William settled down to the job he had been sent to do—Colonel Wallis was still there and threatening to bring suit against the Admiral—and later added another, which his father allowed him to undertake, that of victualing the ships at Kinsale. The war was not going very well; Dutch ships were threatening Irish waters; there must be English ships to protect the coast, and Kinsale Harbor was one of the places where they came to be provisioned.

In January the commissioners for the settlement of Ireland were sitting in London, and the Admiral wrote suggesting that his son "make a step over" to him to see about it. This William was delighted to do. He had been away for a year, and it would be good to see London again—and besides his little sister Pegg was going to be married in February.

He had heard, of course, about the great fire which had swept London in September, but he had not imagined the appalling devastation that he would find there, even after three months. St. Paul's was in ruins—that great, beautiful Gothic cathedral that for centuries had been the center of London life—and seventy-seven other, smaller churches besides. All Hallows at the foot of Seething Lane, where he had been baptized, had been saved only by the energy and quick decision of his father, who sent men with gunpowder into Tower Street to blow up the houses near it. Even so the flames had crept to the very porch and the pillars were blackened with smoke. And all the streets and streets of houses and shops! The piles of ruins still heaped everywhere! The pitiful attempts that the poorer people made to build themselves shelters out of half-burned timbers and broken tiles!

It was a bitterly cold winter, too, and coal cost four pounds a caldron! The suffering everywhere caught at William's heart, even though he tried to close his eyes to what he could not help, and be gay because the commissioners had confirmed Shangarry to his father, and because his sister was going to be married the day after Valentine's Day.

Pegg was fifteen, and Anthony Lowther was twenty-four. It was a quiet wedding at St. Olav's Church, and instead of a wedding dinner they had some friends in for supper a week later, with favors for all the guests to put in their hats. Pegg was very happy, much pleased with a bracelet that Anthony gave her and innocently proud of her dowry of four thousand pounds. She was not going to get her trousseau till after Lent was over, so that she could have everything in the newest summer fashions. William thought it right that with all the suffering in London that winter they should have kept the wedding festivities so simple—but he did wish that they had not borrowed silver plates for the party from the Pepyses. He could *see* Mr. Pepys looking scornfully at the fare, and thinking how sorry it was.

The Lowthers were to stay in London till summer, and then go to Anthony's home in York. William went back to Shangarry to manage the estate which was now all theirs.

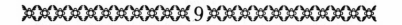

9

Thomas Loe Again

WILLIAM, at Shangarry, needed some articles of clothing and went to Cork to buy them. He went to the same little shop kept by a Quaker woman where his family used to deal when he was a small boy and they lived at Macroom. The shop had prospered. Quakers did well as shopkeepers, for they were known to be honest. Instead of setting a higher price on things than they expected to get, as others did, they had a fixed price and the same price for everybody, and people after they got used to this new system liked it and went out of their way to buy from Quakers.

The woman behind the counter with her plain clothes and serene expression looked just as she had ten years ago when William used to go to the shop with his mother.

"Do you remember me?" he asked.

She searched his face, and shook her head.

"I am the son of Sir William Penn—you came with Thomas Loe to a meeting at Macroom ten years ago."

Her face lighted up. "Oh, now I know thee! To think of thy remembering it! A boy changes much in ten years," she added apologetically.

That meeting at Macroom came back to William with

sudden vividness, and the young man, so serene, so sure, who had stirred them all so deeply. All his own doubts and confusions seemed in that moment to rise up and overwhelm him, and he said impetuously:

"If I knew where that man Loe was, even if it were a hundred miles off, I would go to hear him again!"

The shopkeeper, making a package of the linens he had selected, paused and looked up. "But there is no need to go so far. Thomas Loe is in Cork now, and he will be at the meeting tomorrow."

"Tomorrow? In Cork? Why, then——"

She told him where the meeting was to be held. He rode the fourteen miles back to Shangarry divided in his mind. How strange a coincidence! Could it be that this Thomas Loe had something that he had been seeking—seeking, off and on, for six years now, ever since he was at Oxford? But a Quaker meeting! Among shop-keepers and such-like simple folk. What would his friends at the castle in Dublin think of him? What would his father and his mother say? But his father had said, ten years ago: "Let us be like the noble Bereans and hear him before we judge him."

When he came to the meeting-place next morning and sat down, conspicuous in his feathered hat and wig and Paris suit among the soberly clad Quakers, he looked for Thomas Loe, but did not recognize him till he rose to speak. Then William was startled. Ten years ago he had been a young man; now at thirty-five he was old and broken by hardships and imprisonment. But his eyes were the same, and his shining look, and the compelling quality of his voice.

"There is a faith," he said, "that overcometh the world, and there is a faith that is overcome by the world."

William Penn, sitting there, listening with his whole heart and soul, felt as if those words had been directed straight at him. In George Fox's phrase, they "spoke to his condition." Had he not, during these years of seeking, been overcome again and again by the world? And was he not being shown now a faith that could overcome the world? He listened to Thomas Loe explaining Quaker doctrine of the light within every man's soul, and the way of life of simplicity and self-denial and truth that it revealed, and he felt, deeply and simply, that he had found a faith and a purpose to which he could give himself, wholly and unreservedly, forever.

He hardly knew when meeting was over; a Friend touching his arm brought him back to the day and the room and the movement of people about him.

"I saw thou wast exceedingly reached," said the Friend beside him. "Wouldst thou not like to speak with Thomas Loe?"

The Society of Friends of the Truth, they called themselves, whom the world called Quakers. Waiting beside this gentle, kindly soul till Thomas Loe should be free to speak to him, William felt that their own name for themselves was the true one. Friends of the truth they were, and friends of people too; already he felt understood and accepted.

Thomas Loe remembered the day at Macroom Castle and the boy, the son of the house. He looked keenly at the tall and elegant young man.

"You have made me a Friend of the Truth," said William, feeling that he must put into words at once this conviction that was so strong in him. It seemed as if his life up to now were like a lot of little streams splashing over rocks and losing their way, and as if this hour had joined them all into one deep and strong river that would flow steadily and straight.

"Let us talk further," said Thomas Loe, and they went together to a Friend's house near-by, where, sitting in the inglenook beside a peat fire, the man who had suffered one imprisonment after another until in his fine and ardent face lines of pain and weariness were deeply engraved, tried to tell the eager young worldling what it meant to be a Quaker.

"But I am one now—forever!" cried young William Penn.

Thomas Loe had to be on his way. He must go on to a meeting in another town where he was expected, and his horse, poor beast, was completely worn out. Who could spare a horse for Thomas Loe?

"Take mine," offered William eagerly. It was a chance to put into action the feelings that had so carried him away. "My sumpter horse that I had in France—he will serve you well—and I should feel honored if you would take him."

Kindly but firmly, Thomas Loe refused; neither as a

gift nor a loan would he take William's sumpter horse, and the other Friends agreed with him. William was crestfallen, hurt. They didn't think him enough of a Friend to take his horse.

After his first disappointment had faded, he saw that they were right. He was not yet a Friend. Seriously and unobtrusively, he went about making himself one, proving his sincerity to himself first, and then to others. He went to meeting regularly. He began to learn what it meant to be a consistent Quaker.

It meant, first of all, simplicity and sincerity. It meant saying "thou" and "thee" to one person, since to speak to one man as "you," as if he were two or three men, was to flatter him by suggesting that he was worth two or three. It meant not taking off one's hat to anybody, since men doffed their hats only to those to whom they wished to show a flattering respect, never to poor and humble people. That it meant much more important differences than these, he well understood, but he saw too that by practicing these he could test out his sincerity and prove that he was not ashamed or afraid to show himself to the world as a Quaker.

When a young man of wealth and position suddenly took to calling his elegant friend "thou" and rudely keeping his hat on before men old enough to be his father, it invariably produced one of two effects: laughter or anger. Both were hard to take. It was not easy to be thought ridiculous or boorish by people who used to like and admire him.

All summer William went about the business of his father's estate in Shangarry, and became each day a little more of a Friend. He still wore his fine clothes, for they were what he had, and his wig and his sword (which had saved his life in France without hurting anybody), and he had not yet written to his father about his convincement, dreading too much his anger and disappointment. He was taking one step at a time, but always a step forward into his new faith, never any backward.

Meanwhile the government was tightening the laws against Non-Conformists, those people whose consciences would not allow them to conform to the religion of the Established Church.

On the third of September, when the Friends in their meeting had been gathered into that deep and living silence which was the very essence of their worship, a soldier suddenly burst into the room. The noisiness and the rudeness of the interruption made young William Penn angry—he was not accustomed to being annoyed by common soldiers. Entirely forgetting one of the very first principles of Quakerism, he jumped up, grabbed the soldier by his coat collar, and was about to thrust him violently forth, when a Friend stopped him.

"Nay—nay—we are peaceable folk."

William's hands dropped limply to his sides. He was but a poor Quaker after all. Full of contrition he went back to his bench and sat down. Mingled with his shame was the fear that by his violence he might have got the Friends into trouble.

He was quite right; he had. The soldier, angry in his turn, rushed to the magistrate, and before meeting was over he came back with a troop of constables and more soldiers. William Penn and the other Friends at the meeting were arrested and haled before the Mayor of Cork, a Mr. Timothy Tuckey, on charges of riot and tumultuous assembling.

Mayor Tuckey was amazed to see Sir William Penn's son in his fine clothes among the gray-clad Quakers.

"Mr. Penn, you are no Quaker. If you will give bond for good behavior, you can go free."

"Sir, I *am* a Quaker, and as for giving bond for good behavior, I challenge the world to accuse me justly of the contrary. I have broken no law."

Mayor Tuckey did not care to discuss the legal aspect of it. Into prison William went with the eighteen others, and there, in that cold and crowded and smelly place, he called for pen and ink and proceeded to write to Lord Orrery, his father's friend, once Lord Broghill, who, as President of Munster, could overrule any action of the Mayor of Cork.

It was a long letter that he wrote, and a good one, straightforward and strong, not begging. "Religion, which is at once my crime and mine innocence," he wrote, "makes me a prisoner to the Mayor's malice, but mine own free man." He pointed out that their imprisonment was illegal, and asked that they be released. And furthermore, he declared that a government which allowed people to follow their own religion was actually stronger than one which forced people to go against their consciences. It was his first plea for religious liberty, the great principle for which he was to spend his life.

Lord Orrery, whatever his opinion of religious liberty, thought that the son of an old friend should not be in prison, and he gave an order that William—and the other Friends with him—should be released.

It was a very short imprisonment, but now William knew what it was like to be roughly pushed about by soldiers and constables who once would have bowed down before him; and the Quakers who were with him knew now that he would not flinch when trouble came. He was truly a Friend at last.

It was inevitable that his father should know about it. Before William could bring himself to write to the Admiral, someone else, probably Lord Orrery, had done it for him.

About the middle of October, William heard from his father.

"Son William:

"I hope this will find you in health. The cause of this writing is to charge you to repair to me with all possible speed presently after your receipt of it, and not to make any stay there or any place upon the road until it please God you see me (unless for necessary rest and refreshment).

"Your very afft. father,
"W. Penn."

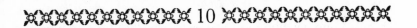

10

Son William and His Father

WILLIAM was not eager to go. One excuse and another he found for delay, until ten days later, a still more peremptory note came from the Admiral.

"Son William:
"I have writ several letters to you since I received any from you. By this I agayne charge you and strictly command that you come with all possible speed. In expectation of your compliance, I remain

"Your afft. father,
"W. Penn."

He took ship from Kinsale and landed at Bristol, where the wharves came deep into the city, and the masts and rigging of boats at anchor mingled with the pointed roofs of houses and clustered chimney pots against the sky. Bristol was his father's city; the Admiral had grown up there, and his mother was buried in the beautiful church of St. Mary Redcliffe. William stayed with his father's friend, Captain George Bishop, who had become a Quaker, and lingered on a day or two to go to meeting —to strengthen himself for the coming tussle.

The Bristol Friends, understanding well that the

newly convinced young Quaker might dread going home
to an Admiral Sir William Penn, suggested that Josiah
Coale, who was going to London anyhow, ride with him
to his father's house. William agreed thankfully. He
knew his father would keep his temper while Josiah
Coale was there, and that first hour or so would be the
most difficult.

The journey to London was much pleasanter than he
had had any idea it could be. Josiah Coale was a comforting person to be with; he too was of a good family and a
fair, though by no means great, estate; and William felt
as they rode steadily along the Great Western Road
through the autumn rains and mist, that his companion
understood and sympathized with the struggle going on
in his heart. He was an interesting person too. Just back
from three years in the American colonies, he had a great
deal to say about that far country: its great forests and
rivers, the clear, cold sunlight, the flaming colors of the
leaves in autumn, the shy, fierce Indians, and the traders
who betrayed and cheated them for gain.

William listened in spite of his preoccupation with
his own concerns. America! If the Friends were to be
scorned and imprisoned and ruined in England, why
should they not go to America and establish the right
kind of government there? An ideal government such as he
used to read about at Oxford, but on Friendly principles.

Sometimes Josiah Coale spoke of his friends, Isaac
and Mary Penington, who lived in Buckinghamshire and
made of their home a haven for all Friends who were in

distress. There was a daughter, by Mary Penington's first marriage, just about William's age—beautiful, gentle, clear-minded Gulielma Springett. Her father had been Sir William Springett, who died in the Civil War just before she was born. Many an ardent young man had gone a-courting her, but she rebuffed them all, kindly but very firmly. Josiah Coale's voice softened as he spoke of Guli Springett, and his eyes were tender.

William was far more interested in the forests and rivers of America than in Guli Springett. The world was full of lovely girls, but where was he to go and what was he to do if his father turned him out?

The Admiral was feeling gloomy and disheartened. His good old friend Sir William Batten had died recently, and he missed him. He himself was suffering tortures with the gout, and the fleet was away without him, being worsted by the Dutch, who had actually sailed up the Thames as far as the Medway River and set fire to the warships anchored there. He had rented a house in Wanstead and was living part of the time there and part of the time in the Navy Gardens. Dick, who was not strong, had gone to Italy for his health; Pegg, barely sixteen, was expecting a baby; and now William had come home a Quaker, or some such melancholy thing. It was too much.

Supper passed off quietly enough; the Admiral said nothing while Josiah Coale was there about William's hat, which remained disrespectfully perched on his wig, or about his studious use of thee and thou. Could he rebuke his son in a guest's presence for doing and saying what the guest himself did and said? But the very first time after Josiah Coale had departed that William said thee to his father, the Admiral exploded.

The young Quaker tried, awkwardly and diffidently, to explain. "But, Father, I do it out of obedience to God, not from any disrespect to thee."

They were alone in the paneled dining-room, which had a fine chimney piece copied from the Pepyses'. The servants had gone to bed; Lady Penn was in Wanstead. The two men, so much alike, faced each other distressed and determined. The Admiral, after visibly struggling with himself, made a magnificent effort and said:

"You may thee and thou whom you please, but three people you may *not* thee and thou—the King, the Duke of York, and myself."

Here was a temptation: to keep his father's friendship by making but three exceptions—and those three, exceptions that anybody might be excused for making. But one who gives way at the first trial on a small point will continue to give way later in large matters. William found himself saying steadily:

"Even to thee, and the King, and the Duke of York, I must speak in the singular manner. It means," he added pleadingly, "no disrespect to—to thee——"

But the Admiral had had all he could stand. Purple with rage, he told his son exactly what he thought of him; and William, who knew even now what he was to write later, that when men are angry is no time to vindicate oneself, for then the true ear is not open to hear it, listened to his father in silence.

As he started up the stairs to bed, the Admiral called after him:

"Son William, I desire you to rise in the morning early, for I would have you go out in the coach with me."

And now William, as he unbuckled his sword and put his wig on its stand, wound his watch, donned his night-cap, and put out the candles in the pewter sconces, was uneasy indeed. Go out in the coach with his father? But where? To court? To court; no doubt that was it. To see if he would wear his hat before the King and say thee to the Duke of York. He tossed and turned in the curtained bed, seeing the contemptuous smiles, the shrugged shoulders, the angry glances of the courtiers, the mounting ire of his father. And that, the last, was the only part of it that he really minded; the other, after all, was a test of courage and sincerity, but this estrangement from his father was a gnawing ache in his heart, an almost unbearable tightness in his throat.

The coach, a very grand one, new since he had been in Ireland, was at the door. William, feeling pale, stepped into it after his father. The horses' hoofs grated on the cobblestones and the heavy coach lurched off, going westward toward Whitehall. The Admiral sat with his hands folded on the head of his cane, and his gouty foot eased on a cushion, and from time to time cleared his throat, but said nothing of where they were going.

At Charing Cross he leaned forward and shouted to the coachman to drive into the park.

William knew now that it was to be a serious talk in private instead of a public test; in some ways, even harder to endure. He waited tensely for his father to speak.

"I have been offered a peerage," said Sir William. "You could be heir to the earldom of Weymouth—but I understand that Quakers do not recognize such titles of nobility."

"No, Father."

"Then there is no use in my accepting it? You are determined on this mad course?"

"Yes, Father, I——"

"It's beyond me what you can be thinking of—trained for a courtier or an ambassador—and turning Quaker! Did you hear about that Quaker who walked naked through the Houses of Parliament with a pan of brimstone on his head, crying out that the end of the world was coming? You have a high station in life, you have had every advantage, and now you are ready to throw it all away. And for what? To be a Quaker, to go among fellows like that!"

It was easy to say that poor Solomon Eccles was a little unbalanced in his zeal, and that it was not the regular practice of Quakers to act as he did, but it was not easy to answer the rest of the argument in terms that would have weight with the bitter and disappointed father. William swallowed twice, and tried.

"It was God, speaking to me in my own conscience.

I can't go against that. It's a cross to me too. I wish I need not disappoint *thee*. But dost thou not remember, ten years ago at Macroom, that meeting with Thomas Loe which thou thyself arranged?" The words came faster now; emotion rose like a tide in the coach; William was getting excited. "Thou wast moved thyself then—I remember tears in thy eyes. I believe thou wast convinced of the truth as well as I—but the grandeur of the world was too great for thee to give up!"

He would have said more, but the Admiral shouted him down. Around and around the park they drove, and around and around in circles went their argument, till each was fathoms deeper than before in his own conviction.

At length the Admiral told the coachman to drive homeward and stop at a tavern on the way. "Suppose we have a glass of wine," he said wearily to William, evidently feeling the need of it.

They had a room to themselves in the tavern, and when the wine was brought, the Admiral suddenly turned and locked the door, an action which threw William into fresh alarm. He remembered with great vividness what happened when he was sent down from Oxford, and he thought that now his father was going to cane him again.

But the Admiral laid his hands on the table, and looking straight at William, his face devastated with grief, said solemnly and heavily:

"I am going to kneel down and pray to God that you may not be a Quaker, nor go ever again to any more of their meetings."

It was too much. In a frenzy of despair young William rushed to the window and flung open the casement.

"Before I will hear thee pray after any such manner," he cried, "I'll leap out of the window!"

Into the quivering silence that followed came a cheerful rat-tat at the door. William, at a nod from his father, went to open it. His hand on the knob trembled.

A titled friend of his father, in feathered hat, lace ruffles, and velvet coat, sailed into the room. "I recognized your coach standing outside," he said genially, "and came up to have a glass of canary with you."

The Admiral and the nobleman swept off their hats to each other. William doggedly kept his on.

"My son," said the Admiral glumly, "is turned Quaker. He uncovers to no one—not even the King himself."

The newcomer, who for all his elegant lace and velvet had a keen face and a kindly one between his long curls, looked from the heavily breathing father to the son, pale and tensely erect, and sized up the situation. Giving William a friendly pat on the shoulder, he turned to the Admiral and said:

"Well, Sir William, I think you may consider yourself happy in a son who can despise the grandeur of the world and refrain from the vices that so many men's sons are running after."

William's gratitude and relief shone out of his eyes, and even the Admiral brightened up a little; it was a new view of the matter, one that had not occurred to him. There might be, he thought, some truth in it.

On the way home they stopped at the house of another friend of his whose opinion he respected, and he too, when the case was put to him, took the sensible view that one's son might very easily go in for something even less desirable than an unfashionable religion. William was much encouraged. He began to hope that he and his father might keep their separate faiths and their love for each other too.

The winter wore on. William stayed away from the parties in the Navy Gardens, and the Navy Office pew in St. Olav's Church knew him no more. He went instead to the new meeting-house which the Friends had built in Gracechurch Street.

Some time during the winter he met George Fox, the shoemaker and shepherd who, alone on Pendle Hill in Westmoreland, had had a vision of a sea of darkness and an infinite ocean of light spreading over the darkness— and through his vision had found the Quaker belief and the Quaker way of life. He was a tall, squarely built, fair-haired man, serene and forthright, a man of great magnetism who drew people irresistibly to him. William, who had given considerable thought to the sword which he still wore, asked George Fox what he ought to do about it, and told him of that episode in Paris.

"Why," said George Fox, "wear it as long as thou canst."

No one but George Fox could have made that answer. The next time they met, George Fox said: "William, where is thy sword?" And William answered: "I took thy advice. I wore it as long as I could."

His wig too he soon gave up. He had gone with another Friend to a meeting in the country, and as they rode along, it suddenly occurred to him that he could not wear that any longer either. He took off his hat, tossed his wig off his head behind him, and rode blithely on without looking back to see what became of it. He felt perceptibly lighter in both heart and head for what he had done.

They went on from one meeting to another, until a magistrate who knew Sir William recognized William among the Quakers, and sent word home that he and others were "causing tumults" by preaching the Quaker doctrine. A letter came promptly from the Admiral, ordering William home again. Reluctantly he went, and as he had done at Bristol, he stopped in London on the way to Wanstead, to strengthen himself by going to a Friends' meeting.

After the meeting, while he was talking to some people there, he saw Josiah Coale coming toward him with a young girl in tow. Full of his own concerns as he was, he recognized in Gulielma Springett, even in that brief meeting, a rare loveliness, of both body and spirit. As he made his way on toward Wanstead, he was thinking about her even more than of his father, of her golden

"Then take your clothes and begone from my house"

hair, and the way she smiled, her gentleness, her air of distinction.

His mother was at Wanstead, and his sister Pegg with her new baby, and his father in a state of mind worse than any he had yet encountered.

There was only a brief introduction to what the Admiral had to say. Would William give up his Quaker ways or would he not?

"Then take your clothes and begone from my house, and I shall dispose of my estate to those who please me better."

It had come, then, to this. William tried to tell his father how truly distressed he was to disappoint him, not because he cared anything about the estate, but because he loved him. He tried to make the Admiral understand that he must be faithful to the truth he knew. But it was no use. His words were empty and meaningless to the man who wanted his beloved son to be a great figure in the world and saw but one path for him to follow to that end.

So William went upstairs to the room that had been his, and packed up a small bundle. Coming down again, he kissed his mother and sister, told his father again that he was sorry to displease him, and so with his bundle and his bursting heart, left his father's house. He heard his mother and Pegg sobbing as he went through the door, and he felt that he had stumbled on a "gloomy and dark day" indeed.

He had not got far when he heard running footsteps behind him. It was the black servant, Jack. He was to come back. Lady Penn said so, and Sir William had gone out of the way.

So Son William went back into the house he had just left forever, and got to his room. He did not see his father at all for several days, and after that he was distant and cold. His mother as always was gentle and sympathetic, but she could not hide her distress.

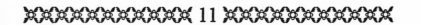

11

"The Sandy Foundation Shaken"

WILLIAM PENN was now twenty-four. He was a young man who did nothing half way. He flung himself heart and soul into the cause of Quakerism.

He preached. He wrote. He went to court with his hat on and pleaded for Quakers who were unjustly in prison. He took part in a debate.

Debates on fine points of religious belief were in that day an extraordinarily popular pastime among middle-class people who did not approve of the theater. They would go and listen breathlessly for hours to harangues on two sides of a question, and at the end, instead of being worn out, would hail the winner with the greatest enthusiasm. There was, for instance, one debate on infant baptism, up in Yorkshire, that lasted all afternoon and all evening, and when it was over the audience rushed down the street shouting joyfully: "Thomas Taylor hath got the day! Thomas Taylor hath got the day!"

The debate in which young William Penn took part came to pass because two members of a Presbyterian chapel in Spitalfields, which was outside the City of London, about a mile north of the Tower, turned Quaker, and their minister Thomas Vincent was so annoyed that

93

he preached with great violence against what he called the "erroneous and damnable doctrines" of the Friends. Whereupon William Penn and George Whitehead, a young London Quaker who had visited the sick in prison all through the plague, challenged Mr. Vincent to a public debate.

The hour was set for two o'clock, but Mr. Vincent privately told his congregation to come at one. When Penn and Whitehead and a few other Friends got there, they found the church jammed full of Vincent's followers, and Vincent already shouting invective against the Quakers. The crowd laughed and hissed and jeered at them as they squeezed their way in and pushed through to the front of the room. When they tried to speak in their own defense, Mr. Vincent's men pulled them down.

Mr. Vincent himself went on talking till it grew dark and the candles had to be lighted. He finished abruptly with a prayer in which, in a whining voice, he called his opponents blasphemers—and since you could be sent to prison for blasphemy, this was a serious charge—and then, without giving them time to reply, declared the meeting over, advised the audience to depart, and led the way by stalking out of the room and up the stairs to the apartment overhead.

He little knew what kind of opponent he had. That was no way to silence William Penn. Up he jumped and launched into his answer. Somebody tried to pull him down and somebody else put out all the candles, but most of the rest waited to listen to this fiery young man who was holding forth with so much eloquence in the chilly, pitch-black room. When Penn sat down, George Whitehead took it up. There was no laughter now, or hissing; whether or not people agreed with or even understood the words that came to them in that compelling voice through the dark, they stayed to hear them.

Some time later, Thomas Vincent came back again, a candle lifted high in his hand. The little pool of light that came in with him shone on his pale face, and on the clear-cut features of the handsome young Quaker, and spread faintly to the people on the front benches. Beyond, all was shadow, dimly moving and rustling.

Mr. Vincent promised that if they would stop now he would meet them again, in another and fairer debate. The long day was over.

It developed, however, that Mr. Vincent had no intention of keeping his promise; he never could find time for that second debate. So Penn wrote his answer in a little book of some thirty-five pages called "The Sandy Foundation Shaken." He always was good at titles.

What he had learned at Saumur, and all that he had thought and felt since then, helped him now, in so short a time, to write out this statement of his belief. He got a man named Richard Derby to print it, and soon everybody was reading it. Even Mr. Pepys, who was much more interested in music than religion, read it—or rather, since his eyes were bothering him, got his wife to read it aloud to him. With the unflattering candor of a neighbor, he said of it: "I find it so well writ as I think it is too good for him ever to have writ it—and it is a serious sort of book and not fit for everybody to read." It was considered very radical by some, and attracted a great deal of attention because of that. People flocked to the Quaker meeting-house where he was likely to appear, in order to see and hear Admiral Penn's Quaker son.

William had made one mistake, however, that turned out to be serious. He entirely forgot about an old law, hardly ever enforced, which required that every book published should be licensed by the Bishop of London. Or perhaps he did not even know about it. At all events, what he did soon learn was that his printer, Richard Derby, was in the Gatehouse prison.

He went immediately to Lord Arlington, the Secretary of State—the same one whom he had seen at Whitehall Palace early that April morning three years before, when he brought dispatches from his father on the *Royal Charles* to the King. (How long ago that seemed, part of another world, and altogether another young man.) He confessed that he had omitted to have the book licensed and asked that the unoffending printer be released and he alone blamed.

It was after all no more than a minor misdemeanor. To his amazement, my Lord Arlington had him arrested forthwith and sent off to the Tower of London without a trial!

At the Tower gate he was met by Sir John Robinson, Lord Lieutenant of the Tower, a man well known in the

Navy Gardens, for he had a private path made specially for him from the Tower to the Navy Office. Mr. Pepys called him a "talking, bragging, buffle-headed fellow," but the Admiral liked him. Sir John refused to receive a prisoner into the Tower without a legal warrant signed by the King in council. Such a warrant was as a rule issued only for treasonable conduct, not for misdemeanors, but young William Penn's book, "The Sandy Foundation Shaken," had deeply offended the Bishop of London, who applied the dread word blasphemous to it. Furthermore, Lord Arlington had a soft spot in his heart for the Presbyterians, against whom William had debated— and for some time had cherished a private spite against Admiral Penn. King Charles, who was entirely friendly to his old Admiral, perhaps thought he would do him a good turn by curing his son of his Quakerism with a stiff dose of the Tower. And so, for a mixture of motives and reasons, a warrant was signed on December 16 by the King and six of his Council, commanding that William Penn be held a close prisoner till the King's pleasure was further signified. One of the six who signed it was the Duke of Ormonde, who only a little over a year before had been so friendly to William in Dublin. Truly he must have felt bewildered and hurt as the gates of the Tower of London clanged to behind him.

His father was ill and sent no word.

12

In the Tower of London

Most political prisoners in the Tower of London were allowed a certain amount of liberty: their friends might come to see them, they could buy the food and drink and extra comforts that they needed, they could walk in the Tower gardens for fresh air and exercise, and occasionally go out on parole. Even such imprisonment as this in the Tower which had so grim and ghastly a history was severe enough; Admiral Penn had been well-nigh broken in spirit and health by five weeks of it.

But young William Penn was in "close confinement," which meant that he never left his tiny room high up under the roof, and was never alone in it; a keeper was always there. He might see no one, not even a doctor or a barber, without a special license. He could write no letters and receive no presents. He had to eat the unappetizing and scanty food provided by the prison, and tried to keep warm in this coldest of winters, when the Thames was frozen over for the first time in years, with the meager bits of fuel that were allowed him. And he was given not the slightest idea how long this imprison-

*"My prison shall be my grave before I will budge one jot,
for I owe my conscience to no man"*

ment was to last. Perhaps for years. Men could die forgotten in the Tower.

His father was ill at Wanstead; he had given up his
post in the Navy Board and his house in the Navy Gardens. Peace had been made with the Dutch, in a compro-
mising sort of treaty whereby Holland kept her islands
in the East Indies, which England had hoped to get, and
the Duke of York acquired the Dutch colonies in America, which nobody cared very much about. The Admiral

was only forty-eight, but he was a broken and disappointed old man, and ill; he stayed in Wanstead nursing his gout and his grief and waiting to see what effect the Tower would have upon his Quaker son.

Thomas Loe and Josiah Coale, the Friends who had so influenced and helped William, had both died that autumn. George Whitehead, and the Peningtons, who were coming to mean more and more in his life, were not allowed to visit him in the Tower. The only person he was permitted to see—and only in the presence of his keeper—during all those dark, icy, winter months, was his servant Francis Cooke.

Cooke brought no message from William's father, only an ominous and disheartening piece of news: the Bishop of London had said that he was resolved that Penn should "either publicly recant, or die a prisoner."

With magnificent courage young William Penn made answer. "All is well. I wish they had told me so before, since the expecting of a release put a stop to some business. Thou mayest tell my father, who I know will ask thee, these words: that my prison shall be my grave before I will budge a jot, for I owe my conscience to no mortal man."

The "business" which had been interrupted by unfounded hopes, he took up again. William Penn was not the man to sit and mope, no matter how cold or how despairing he was. All the energy that might have gone into raging helplessly against the injustice and the senselessness of his imprisonment, he put instead into the book that he had set himself to write. "No Cross, No Crown" was the name of it, a title suggested by Thomas Loe's farewell words to him: "Dear heart, bear thy cross; and God will give thee an eternal crown of glory that no one shall ever take from thee." When finished, the book was a hundred and eleven pages long, and it was good. Since 1669 it has gone into fifty editions, and for more than two hundred and fifty years people have found strength and inspiration in it. But not William's father, who said gloomily that it was certainly a cross to him.

Francis Cooke did not come back again to the little, damp, cold room where his young master sat day after day covering sheets of paper with his large sprawling handwriting and trying not to think that he might spend the rest of his life doing the same thing in the same place. Cooke went to see various Quakers in London, collected forty pounds from them, which he said would be used for Penn's relief, and then absconded with the money. Not till much later did William learn about it, and then he paid back every penny to those who had given it; but he could not pay himself back for his disappointment in the man he had trusted, or for the pain of watching, day after long day, for the friend and servant who did not come.

His father came at last. In April when in Wanstead daffodils were in bloom and the chaffinches were singing in the hedges, the Admiral came to his son's room in the Tower, where spring made no sign at all, and begged

CARL A. RUDISILL LIBRARY
LENOIR-RHYNE COLLEGE

him to take back what he had written, and to give up his
Quakerism. Once again William refused, wondering a
little perhaps at his father's blindness. Could he really
think that William would recant?

Then the Admiral went to court and petitioned that
his son be brought to trial. The Council refused. The
best it could do for him was to direct that the Bishop of
London, Dr. Humphrey Henchman, should examine William Penn and judge of his views for heresy.

The Bishop, instead of going himself, sent Dr. Edward Stillingfleet to talk to William and endeavor to
change his opinions.

Dr. Stillingfleet was the most fashionable and successful young divine in London; only thirty-four, he was
rector of St. Andrew's, Holborn, lecturer at the Temple,
canon of St. Paul's, author of several books on theology,
and the most popular preacher at Whitehall. He and
Penn liked each other immediately, and during that long,
slow spring when the room under the tiles gradually
stopped being damp and icy and became damp and stuffy,
these few and brief visits were all that William had to
look forward to.

Dr. Stillingfleet took great pains with the attractive
but stubborn young Quaker whom he liked so much,
and William warmed to his kindness and delighted in
his learning. After months of the incessant company of
a stupid and grunting jailer, it was more than refreshing
to talk to so wise and witty and kind a gentleman. But all
the doctor's arguments, and all his "moving and inter-

CARL A. RUDISILL LIBRARY
LENOIR-RHYNE COLLEGE

esting motives of the King's favor and preferment" had no effect whatsoever on William's opinions.

"Thou canst tell the King," said Penn with finality, "that the Tower is the worst argument in the world to convince me. Whoever is in the wrong, those who use force in religion can never be in the right."

So Dr. Stillingfleet went back and told the King exactly that. A young man who could speak thus after seven months of close confinement in the Tower was not to be easily intimidated, or bluffed into recanting.

Just to make sure that his conviction of the ridiculousness of trying to change men's ideas about the future life by shutting them up without enough food or fresh air in this life was being known, Penn wrote a letter to Lord Arlington in which he said that force might make hypocrites but not converts, and pointed out that the great nations of ancient times—Greece, Egypt, Rome—thrived on religious toleration.

Then thinking over what Dr. Stillingfleet had said about people's having misunderstood what he had written in "The Sandy Foundation Shaken," he wrote another pamphlet, in which he stated all the same opinions over again, but explained more clearly what he really meant by them. He called this "Innocency with Her Open Face." By this time his little room under the roof was intolerably hot. The sun baked down on the lead roof close over his head, and scarcely any air came in through the little high window.

Meanwhile the Admiral, who could recognize and respect courage when he saw it, had gone to his old friend, the Duke of York, and begged him to help his son; and the Duke of York went to the King.

The Council sat again at the end of July. Dr. Stilling-fleet made his report; "Innocency with Her Open Face" was produced. The King declared himself satisfied, and ordered Sir John Robinson to release the prisoner and deliver him to his father. There was some further delay, but finally, after nearly nine months in the Tower of London, young William Penn was free.

Snow had been in the streets and ice on the river when he went in; now it was hot and dusty and a few yellow leaves drifted out of the trees. But the sky! The river! The fresh sweet breeze, and the sunshine! The space all around him! Long vistas down streets, and people walking where they pleased! For a few moments he stood drinking in his freedom in great gulps. Thoughts of all the things he could do now that he was free came crowding joyfully in upon him. Nothing could stop him now!

And one of the very first things he would do would be to go and see Gulielma Springett.

13

A Year in a Young Man's Life

Lovely Guli Springett had many suitors. She was beautiful, she was an heiress, she was sweet and gentle —and spirited. From "every rank and condition," as we know from Thomas Ellwood, who also loved her, came ardent young men to beg her to marry them, and each in his turn she refused. She was twenty-five years old, a considerable age in those days when girls married at fifteen, before "he for whom she was reserved" came riding out from London, the prison pallor still in his face but the light of joy in his gray-blue eyes.

Bury Farm, all Tudor brick and pointed gables and moss-grown tiled roofs, sat under its chestnut trees at the point where the road from Beaconsfield met the road from London and became the High Street of the village of Amersham. Behind it was Gore Hill, and in front of it, across the Misbourne River, was another hill, patterned with green fields and hedges and patches of beechwoods. To one side over the roofs of Amersham rose the gray tower of the flint church where John Knox had preached a hundred years or so before: "steeplehouse" was the Quaker word for it.

They were all Quakers at Bury Farm: Isaac Penington,

who had spent five out of the last nine years in prison for his religion; Mary Penington, his wife and Guli's mother, who after long years of "weary seeking and not finding" had found her spiritual home in the Society of Friends; Gulielma Springett, who had been convinced at fourteen; and the three Penington children, her half-brothers, who were born into Quakerism. Thomas Ellwood, five years older than Guli, had also been one of the family almost continuously since his father, Squire Ellwood of Crowell, had cast him out for refusing hat-honor. After a brief period in London, when he was secretary to the blind poet Milton, he had come to the Peningtons as Latin tutor for the younger children, and stayed on as right-hand man of affairs. The Peningtons' home—whether it was the Grange in Chalfont St. Peter, or Bury Farm, their temporary quarters in Amersham, or Woodside, where they later lived—was always a haven for Friends who were in distress of mind or condition, and their spirit went out over the countryside.

To Bury Farm came William Penn on the sixteenth of September 1669. He was on his way to Ireland. His father, who still refused to see him, had given orders through Lady Penn that Son William was to go to Ireland and administer the Shangarry estate. There were a great many people at Bury Farm when he got there; two Friends had ridden out from London with him, and other Friends from the neighborhood gathered to see the visitors; a meeting was held in the farm parlor. Guli was there, lovely and serene and a little remote; it was hard to talk to her with so many people about; and of course he must not think about her during the meeting for worship. The next morning he said his farewells, and rode away, through Beaconsfield, to Maidenhead.

There, the servant whom he had expected to find waiting for him failed to show up. In high feather he wheeled around and galloped back to Amersham. That was the seventeenth. On the eighteenth he and Guli rode to Penn Street, a little village about half way between Amersham and Penn, where his distant cousins lived. No doubt they had an errand to do there, for Mary Penington gave counsel and help to half the countryside, but William wrote nothing of that in his journal; just that they went there. Nor did he write down what they talked about, though they must have said many things that they were to remember all their lives. Perhaps they tried to think back to their childhood and to recall whether they had ever seen each other in Chigwell, when William went to the Grammar School there and Guli used to visit her step-grandfather, Alderman Penington, who had lived in the big brick house on Chigwell Street.

The next day William and Guli and some others walked to Russby, to a meeting there, and William wrote to Aylesbury for his servant. Early in the morning of the twentieth the servant came, and there was no longer any good excuse for tarrying. Isaac and Mary Penington were both going to Reading to visit, and they would ride along with William, whose way to Bristol lay through Reading. Guli rode with them a little beyond

Maidenhead, and Thomas Ellwood came along to escort her back.

And so they parted, these two who knew now that they loved each other. It would be nearly a year before they saw each other again, and two years more before they could be married.

It took two days to ride from Reading to Bristol. There Penn stayed for nearly a month, visiting different Friends and attending meetings. On the twenty-fourth of October, the wind being east northeast, he set sail, and two days later, through the autumn, he saw the fields of Shangarry rising out of Cork Harbor.

He went first to Cork, where he found most of the Friends in prison, put there, as he wrote in his journal, "as much from envy about trade as for zeal for religion." He visited the jail and found that they had made of it "a meeting-house and work-house, for they would not be idle anywhere." He had a meeting with them there, and dined with them on their prison fare, and afterwards he went to see the Mayor to plead for their release, but it was no use. So off he went to Dublin, to exert his influence there, spending one night on the way at Rosenalla, the farm where William Edmundson lived, the man who was the first Quaker in Ireland. Another night he spent at Thurles, the ancient manor house of the Duke of Ormonde.

His whole time in Ireland was like that: one day supping in prison and the next dining at court.

The Duke of Ormonde was no longer the Lord Lieu-

tenant of Ireland; he had run up against the Cabal, the
powerful group of men that was ruling England, and he
had been worsted by them. But the Penns' old friend,
Lord Orrery, whom William still called Lord Broghill
because it was so as a boy he first knew him, was in
Dublin, and his younger brother Lord Shannon. Lord
Arran was there, whom he so loved and admired, and
Lord Sheffield who had studied at Saumur only a few
years before William did. They all made him welcome,
in spite of his Quakerism, and even helped him to help
the Friends in their difficulties.

He took lodgings in Dublin with John and Ann Gay,
and stayed there for the whole month of November. The
general half-yearly meeting for Ireland met in his lodgings on the fifth, and he helped them to draw up an account of the sufferings of the Quakers to be presented to
the Lord Lieutenant. Most of that month Penn spent in
pleading with the influential men he knew for mercy and
justice for his oppressed people, and he soon became a
well-known figure in Dublin. Such a handsome young
man, with so many friends at court—and yet a Quaker!
He was a wonder to the common people and a joke among
the stupider of his own class. One Sunday some of the
"ruder boisterous gallants" of the city came to meeting
just to stare at him, which, he said, "they did for almost
an hour." When meeting was over, he spoke to them
"very sharply."

He wrote a good many letters during that month: to
his father, to George Whitehead, to Isaac and Mary Pen-

ington, to George Fox, who had recently married Margaret Fell of Swarthmore Hall—and to Guli Springett.

At last he got an order in council for the release of all the Quakers who were in prison in Dublin, and satisfied for the present, he turned southward again to Shangarry to attend to his father's business. It took six days in that wet and wintry weather, and it was not easy going.

Ferrying across the Blackwater River, J.P., his companion, fell overboard and was almost drowned in the swift deep icy water. The boatman and Penn both rushed to catch him, the boat tipped, the horses slid down on top of them, and for a little while it looked as if Penn, the boatman, the horses, and the ferry-boat were all going to land on top of the floundering man in the Blackwater River. Just in time they caught their balance, and everything was all right. They went on as fast as they could to an inn, where Penn put J.P. to bed with hot drinks while his clothes were being dried. Nothing was lost but J.P.'s hat and two hours' time.

The winter he spent at Imokilly, finding tenants for his father's farms and arranging terms and leases, writing to Guli and watching eagerly for the rare packets in which came letters to him from Guli, from his father, or his sister Pegg, or his younger brother Dick.

Once he went to Kinsale, where he stayed at the Green Dragon Inn while he arranged to sell the posts of governor of the town and captain of the fort and garrison, which his father owned, to his cousin Richard Rooth for four hundred pounds. How long ago those days seemed when Captain Rooth wrote to Admiral Penn about William's courage at Carrickfergus, and William wrote and begged his father to make over to him the captaincy of Kinsale! Things had happened in those three years that neither the Admiral nor Son William could have foreseen.

During those gray, wet, wintry days William, undaunted by the results of "The Sandy Foundation Shaken," took to writing again. He wrote a "Letter of Love to the Young Convinced," in which he said: "Neither let us enter into many reasonings with the opposers," and then with great energy began at once to reason with the opposers himself in a pamphlet that he called "The Great Case of Liberty of Conscience." He was putting into it some of those thoughts about religious liberty that had come to him in the Tower, and it was too strong and deep a thing for him to finish hastily. He needed more time and more thought for it, but it was well begun in Ireland.

Early in May, a letter came from his father which brought him uneasiness and yet thankfulness too. The Admiral wrote: "I wish you had well done all your business there, for I find myself to decline." He knew now that he was forgiven, and that his father wanted him to come home.

By the end of May he had finished the Shangarry business, but he wished to make things easier for the Friends in Cork before he left. The mayor being still unco-operative—"a wickeder mayor or judge had not been in the city of Cork since Truth came"—he made a flying trip to Dublin, riding all night long to get there, and once more called upon his powerful friends to help him.

They stood by him nobly. They had accepted the fact now that he was a Friend and they liked him for his charm and his courage and his loyalty. Lord Arran took him in his coach to court, and presented his petition for him, and afterwards, as an act of real fellowship, went to a Friends' meeting with him.

The next day all the Quaker prisoners in Ireland were set free. Penn gave a farewell dinner party in his lodgings to Lord Arran, Lord Shannon, and Lord Sheffield; and gave Lord Arran a parting gift of a horse. (How often they had gone for wild gallops together in those long-past days, three years ago, when Lord Arran was the son of the viceroy of Ireland, and young William Penn was a courtier and—almost—a soldier.)

In the middle of June William Penn set out for England. He was going back to his father at last.

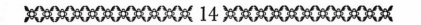

14

Turmoil in Gracechurch Street

SUNDAY the fourteenth of August 1670 was one of the most important days in all of William Penn's life. Not that he had any idea of that as he rode briskly away from Wanstead early in the morning to go to meeting in London.

What he did know was that it was a time of struggle and of testing for all Quakers and that more than ever it was dangerous to be one. The Conventicle Act, which Parliament had passed a few months before, had let loose upon the land a very tornado of persecution. It was intended to wipe out all religious denominations except the Established Church, but it hit the Quakers hardest. Some of the forbidden sects avoided trouble by holding their meetings in secret or at odd hours, but the Friends of the Truth met openly at their regular times and in their regular places. When their meeting-houses were padlocked, they met outside in the street; when they were burned, they met on the ruins; when haled off to jail, they went submissively but refused to pay the fines, which they said were unjust; and while they waited patiently in prison to be released, the children, in some places, went right on with the meetings.

He knew that Isaac Penington was in jail in Reading and that Gulielma was worried and distressed because her beloved step-father was not strong enough physically to endure very much such hardship. He knew that George Fox was ill in Stratford, and that Margaret his wife could not go to him because she was in prison in Lancaster.

He knew very well that he himself might spend that very night in jail instead of going happily back to his father's house at Wanstead. He pushed that thought out of his mind; he did not want to think of being separated from his father now. They had had two months together since William's return from Ireland, a time of love without reserve, and understanding and respect. There had not been a cloud between them, except the Admiral's failing health. Sir William Penn was only forty-nine, but he had lived strenuously and he was now almost worn out. Son William, riding to London to meeting this Sunday morning, pushed away the thought that he might be arrested before night. The thought that he might remain safely at home instead never occurred to him.

The big new meeting-house which the Friends had built since the Great Fire stood in White Hart Court off Gratechurch Street. When William got there, he found the meeting-house padlocked and Friends already gathering outside the doors. Presently there were so many that they overflowed the little court into Gracechurch Street itself. Other people were there too besides the Quakers, rude folk who drifted in from Fenchurch Street and East Cheap to see what was going on. They stood about the fringes of the group, craning their necks, pushing and shoving, talking noisily. Soon a troop of musketeers and watchmen armed with halberds, a sort of cross between a spear and a battle-ax, arrived, and in their train still more of the rabble, delighted with the prospect of excitement.

There were now, packed together in the hot street, four or five hundred people. Over their heads the watchmen's halberds stuck up into the air and caught the sun on their blades.

It was a strange sort of Friends' meeting, far removed from that one at Macroom long ago, or those at Bury Farm when the room was filled with peace and love, and Guli Springett sat on the window-seat. There was no peace here, no silence; but there were Quakers who had come in spite of danger, and there might be among the rude and idle strangers one or two whom Truth in some unforeseen way might reach. Calmly, knowing full well that the soldiers were waiting just for this moment, William Penn mounted onto a doorstep and began to speak.

At once the musketeers and watchmen began to force their way through the tightly packed crowd toward him. He saw the pain and dread on the faces of those whom they roughly jostled and thrust aside on their way.

"Let me finish," he shouted, "and I will go with you when meeting is over."

He saw a man speak with their captain, and saw him nod and stand still. Some of the sightseers grumbled; somebody cried out: "Silence." Above the din William

Penn shouted the message that he felt he had to give.

He could not be sure that anyone heard it, or that, in all the confusion and turmoil, they had any real attention to give to it. But soldiers or no soldiers, a meeting there should be, and young Penn thundered his belief in God's voice in the silence at the top of his lungs to the very last syllable before he turned and gave himself up to the soldiers.

He found that they had a firm grip on another man too, a man whom he had never seen before.

"I gave myself as surety for thee," he said. "William Mead is my name."

"Now that I am here, thou canst go free——"

Surely that was good sense. But the soldiers marched them both away, a crowd streaming after them to see what was going to happen.

That evening they were taken before the Lord Mayor, along with a little band of Independents and Baptists who, with Penn and Mead, made up the day's catch of Non-Conformists. A crowd of a hundred or so gathered to watch the fun.

Sir Samuel Starling was the Lord Mayor. Making no motion to remove his hat, William Penn looked straight into the cold and angry eyes of the man who was king within the City of London. He knew that the Mayor was expecting him, for the warrant that the soldiers bore had been made out beforehand with the name of William Penn; he knew that for some obscure reason Sir Samuel Starling had a grudge against his father; he knew that

Starling, having been once a violent supporter of Cromwell, now was making a bid for the King's favor by being
still more violent against Non-Conformists. "Truly,"
thought William, "the old saying is right. One renegade
is worse than three Turks."

The Lord Mayor began by having a soldier yank William's hat off his head.

"You shall have it pulled off," he said disagreeably,
"for all you are Admiral Penn's son."

"I wish to be treated like any other Quaker," replied
William equably. "I seek no refuge from the common
usage."

"It makes not the slightest difference if your father
was a commander twenty years ago," pursued the Mayor.

William, preferring to leave his father out of it, began
to explain the Quaker attitude about hat-honor, but the
Mayor would not listen. He had more to say about the
Admiral, ugly slurs that stung young William Penn to
hot retort:

"I can bear anything you say about me, but you have
no right to abuse my father, when he is not here to defend himself."

A murmur of approval went through the crowd behind him, and the Lord Mayor brought the session to
an abrupt close. He committed Penn, and Mead too, as
rioters forthwith.

That night they spent at the Sign of the Black Dog, in
Newgate Market, a dirty and unsavory little inn where
prisoners were sometimes lodged temporarily. From

there William wrote next morning to his father an account of the whole affair, winding up:

"And now, dear father, be not displeased or grieved. ... I doubt not I may be at liberty in a day or two to see thee. I am very well and have no trouble upon my spirits, besides my absence from thee, especially at this juncture, but otherwise I can say I was never better; and what they have to charge me with is harmless."

But he was not out in a day or two. He and Mead were taken to Newgate Prison, where they spent the next two weeks awaiting trial.

Newgate was one of the gates in the old city wall, and the prison, which was built over and about the gate, had been in use since the days of King John and the Magna Carta. Penn had seen it often enough from the outside. Over the gate on the eastern side were niches with statues of Justice, Fortitude, and Prudence; on the western side were Liberty, with Dick Whittington's cat at her feet, Security, and Plenty; a curious collection of virtues to be associated with this revolting old jail where injustice and insecurity and destitution and oppression permeated the very stones. The tower on one side was the Master's side, where prisoners could pay rent and have somewhat more private but by no means clean or comfortable quarters; the other tower was the common side where the prisoners were crowded at night into a single round room with a great oak pillar in the center that supported the chapel above. They slung their hammocks all around the pillar, between it and the opposite

Newgate Prison

wall, in three stories, one above the other. Those who went to bed earliest slept in the top tier, and those who were left over slept on the floor. There were sometimes nearly a hundred people there, thieves and murderers and vagabonds and innocent men, sick and well, all mixed up, crowded into a round room as wide across as the length of two hammocks and the thickness of the pillar. Over the gateway between the two towers was the common hall where the prisoners could walk in the daytime and beg out of the windows for money and food. It was, altogether, a disgusting and unhealthy place.

Here Penn and Mead made friends with each other and prepared for their trial. William Mead, who had been a captain in Cromwell's army when he was twenty, was now, at forty-one, a prosperous London citizen, a linen-draper, a bachelor, and a recently convinced Friend. He had heard much about William Penn and looked up to him, for all Penn was fifteen years younger.

They had a great deal to think about, the two Williams in those August days. A trial loomed ahead of them, but they were allowed no counsel for their defense, no lawyer to plead for them. They could have nobody to advise them before the trial, no one to speak for them at the trial. They could have no books to help them work up their own defense. They were not allowed to make any arrangements about producing witnesses in their own behalf. They had no inkling of the line the prosecution was going to take against them, except that they were to be accused of riot and conspiracy, which was obviously absurd. Worst of all, they knew very well that though they were to be tried before a jury, they could not be sure that the jury would dare to say what it really thought. Ever since Tudor times and the days of the Star Chamber, juries that brought in verdicts unpleasing to the judges had been disciplined by fine or imprisonment till they knew better. And because of that juries were pretty apt to bring in the verdict that they thought the judges would like rather than that which they believed to be true.

Day after day they talked together in that hot, crowded smelly place, while their fellow prisoners grumbled and quarreled and begged around them. Day after day William Penn, who had studied at Lincoln's Inn, coached William Mead in the common law. Lucky for him now that he knew Coke's *Institutes* almost by heart, knew the Magna Carta and what it meant to Englishmen.

"There are certain ancient fundamental laws of England," he would say again and again, "that relate to liberty and property and are not limited to particular persuasions in the matter of religion. On these we must take our stand. And the jury are our judges, not the magistrates on the bench."

Brave words. But would the jury stand firm? Would they dare oppose Sir Samuel Starling, who would be the Chief Justice?

The August days crept past in the heat and smells and dirt and noise of the over-crowded old jail, and William Penn labored to remember everything he had ever learned about the law, and by teaching it to William Mead learned it the more firmly himself. And all the time, he knew, his mother and father were grieving for him, and his father's life was slipping away. And Gulielma? Yes, Guli too was troubled for him, he was sure of it. But that was a thought that brought strength and comfort with it.

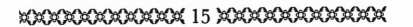

15

The Trial

O N THURSDAY the first of September 1670, a sergeant and his yeomen came early in the morning to escort Penn and Mead out of Newgate and down the street called the Old Bailey to the Sessions House, where the court sat at seven. It was a "fair and stately building," with large galleries for spectators.

There were ten justices on the bench. Several of them young William Penn already knew. Sir Samuel Starling was Chief Justice. The Admiral's "buffle-headed" old friend, Sir John Robinson, the Lord Lieutenant of the Tower, was another—and good reason William had for remembering him! A third, Sir Richard Brown, had been particularly brutal in his raids on the Friends' meeting-houses a few years ago, and two more were well known as zealous churchmen and persecutors of Non-Conformists. Altogether they were about as arrogant, puffing, choleric, muddleheaded, prejudiced a lot of judges as one could find anywhere.

The jury was sworn in, twelve slow-witted, plain citizens, with good plain English names, John and James and William and Henry. There was an Edward Bushell, and Thomas Veer was foreman.

The prisoners were brought before the bar, and the indictment read. It was an astonishing piece of writing: a single sentence of two hundred and fifty words looped and bunched together in alternately legal and hysterical phrases. The gist of it was that "William Penn, gent., and William Mead, linen-draper, the fifteenth day of August, with force and arms unlawfully and tumultuously did assemble, and the aforesaid William Penn by agreement between him and William Mead before made, then and there in the open street did take upon himself to preach and speak, by reason whereof a great concourse and tumult of people in the street, a long time did remain and continue in contempt of the Lord the King and of his law, to the great disturbance of his peace and to the great terror of many of his liege subjects."

The Clerk then asked: "What say you, William Penn and William Mead? Are you guilty as you stand indicted, or not guilty?"

They pleaded "Not guilty," and the court was adjourned till afternoon.

While they were waiting, they discussed the errors in the indictment. To begin with, the date was wrong; the day of the meeting was Sunday the fourteenth of August, not the fifteenth. In the second place, they did not meet with force and arms. Nobody had arms except the soldiers. Nobody used force except the soldiers. Then, since they had never seen each other before, they obviously could not have met by agreement before made. And finally, they did not remain and continue in contempt of the King and his law, for the chief officer who came to take them had allowed the meeting to go on after Mead promised that Penn would go with them at the end of it.

In the afternoon they were brought back to the Sessions House, but instead of going on with their trial, the court, "both to affront and to tire them," kept them waiting there for five long hours while trials of felons and murderers were held, and at the end of the time adjourned.

September second they cooled their heels in Newgate.

September third was a Saturday. The sergeant and his yeomen came for them again before seven. Just as they went into the courtroom one of the officers, on a kindly impulse, took off their hats for them. Sir Samuel Starling was quick to see.

"Sirrah," he thundered, "who bid you put their hats off? Put them on again."

So, hats on, they stood before the bar. Ten judges in wigs and robes sat in a portentous row upon the bench and looked down with hostile eyes, while the chief among them proceeded solemnly to fine the prisoners forty marks apiece for wearing their hats in court.

It was childish; it was contemptible. William Penn, who was twenty-five, looked straight into all those hard and prejudiced old eyes, and said calmly: "I desire it may be observed that we came into the court with our hats off (that is, taken off), and if they have been put on since, it was by order from the Bench, and therefore not we, but the Bench, should be fined."

There being no answer to that, the jury was sworn
again. Sir John Robinson objected to the way Edward
Bushell took the oath. Bushell was known to be a man of
tender conscience and tough will, and the judges were a
little uneasy about him. They had no good excuse, however, for getting rid of him, and so the trial went forward.

The first witness was called and sworn to tell "the
truth, the whole truth, and nothing but the truth, so help
me God."

Lieutenant Cook, in command of the soldiers, testified
that he saw Mr. Penn speaking to the people but could
not hear what he said. Two others said that they saw
Penn preaching to some four hundred people and Mead
talking to Lieutenant Cook, but could not hear what
either Penn or Mead said. There was no further evidence.

Then Penn spoke up and said: "I desire you would let
me know by what law it is you prosecute me, and upon
what law you ground my indictment."

The Recorder of London, who was the legal expert on
the case, answered promptly: "The common law."

At once Penn asked: "What is that common law?" but
the legal expert could not produce a definition or an
example of it. The other justices on the bench began to
shout at Penn, and the Recorder snapped:

"The question is whether you are guilty of this indictment."

Penn corrected him. "The question is not whether I
am guilty of this indictment, but whether the indictment
be legal." He pointed out that if the common law was so

hard to understand it was very far from being common, and he quoted Coke and the Magna Carta.

The Recorder, losing his temper completely, shouted: "Sir, you are an arrogant fellow, and it is not for the honor of the court to suffer you to go on!" To which Penn answered mildly: "I have asked but one question, and you have not answered me; though the rights and privileges of every Englishman are concerned in it."

"If I should suffer you to ask questions till tomorrow morning," replied the Recorder huffily, "you would never be the wiser."

And young Penn could not resist the temptation to retort: "That is according as the answers are.

That was too much for the judges; they turned purple with rage.

"I desire no affront to the court but to be heard in my just plea. . . ."

The Mayor and the Recorder both broke out in indignant shouts: "Take him away! Take him away! Turn him into the bale-dock."

The bale-dock was a sort of pen at the far end of the courtroom, open at the top but enclosed by high palings so that the prisoners could not see or hear what was going on. Before he was dragged off to this coop, William Penn delivered a ringing challenge:

"Is this justice or true judgment? Must I therefore be taken away because I plead for the fundamental laws of England? However, this I leave upon your consciences, who are of the jury and my sole judges, that if these ancient fundamental laws which relate to liberty and property (and are not limited to particular persuasions in the matter of religion) must not be indispensably maintained and observed, who can say he hath a right to the coat upon his back?"

"Be silent there."

"I am not to be silent in a case wherein I am so much concerned, and not only myself but many ten thousand families besides."

Roughly they pulled him off to the bale-dock. Mead had his turn, stood his ground well, quoted a Latin tag, defined a riot, and was also consigned for his pains to the bale-dock.

There, stuck away in the dimness, they could not hear what was going on in the court, but one of the officers whispered to them that the Recorder was charging the jury. It was absolutely against the law to charge the jury in the absence of the prisoners. Penn flung himself on the palings and pulled himself up so that he could shout over the top of them:

"I appeal to the jury who are my judges!" Loudly as he could, he quoted the law, and he called to the jury to take notice that he had not been heard in his own defense.

"Pull that fellow down, pull him down," bawled the Recorder.

The people in the galleries craned their necks and rustled and buzzed.

"I say these are barbarous and unjust proceedings!"

shouted Penn, clinging to the side of the bale-dock.

"Take them away to the hole," commanded the Recorder.

To the hole they went, a sort of dungeon in the Sessions House, a stinking hole, Penn said, and one that the Lord Mayor would not consider a fit sty for his swine. There they stayed while the jury deliberated.

They were a long time at it. After an hour and a half, eight of them returned to the court, and four who disagreed remained in the jury chamber above. The four, of whom Edward Bushell was recognized as the leader, were brought down and scolded and threatened by the court. All twelve of them were then sent back to reach a conclusion, and this time, after more deliberation, they brought the unanimous verdict that William Penn was guilty of speaking in Gracechurch Street.

This of course was equal to an acquittal. There was no law against speaking in Gracechurch Street. The Mayor tried to make them say "speaking to an unlawful assembly," but they refused. Determined to have a different verdict, he ordered them back to the jury chamber, and they asked for pen, ink, and paper to take with them.

In a little more than half an hour they returned, Penn and Mead were brought back to the bar, and the jury handed in its verdict again, this time written and signed. "We do find William Penn to be guilty of speaking or preaching to an assembly met together in Gracechurch Street, the fourteenth of August last, 1670, and that

William Mead is not guilty of the said indictment."

Whereupon the Mayor called Bushell "an impudent, canting fellow," and the Recorder told them all:

"Gentlemen, you shall not be dismissed till we have a verdict the court will accept; and you shall be locked up without meat, drink, fire, and tobacco. You shall not think thus to abuse the court; we will have a verdict, or by the help of God you shall starve for it."

Before the jury departed again, Penn got his word in, and the voice of this young man of twenty-five, whom the Lord Mayor later called "that wild, rambling colt," was the only calm and authoritative voice in the whole amazing, hysterical courtroom.

"My jury, who are my judges, ought not to be thus menaced. Their verdict should be free and not compelled. The bench ought to wait upon them but not forestall them."

But the court was ready to break up for the day and "huddle the prisoners to the jail and the jury to their chamber." As the second day of the trial ended, Penn turned to the jury and said:

"You are Englishmen; mind your privileges, give not away your right."

To which Bushell stanchly made reply: "Nor will we ever do it."

And that night the jury was shut up without "meat, drink, fire, nor any other accommodation."

The next day was Sunday, and it was illegal to hold court. Nevertheless, at seven, the court sat.

The foreman of the jury read the verdict again: "William Penn is guilty of speaking in Gracechurch Street."

The Mayor prompted him: "To an unlawful assembly?" and Edward Bushell answered for him: "No, my lord, we give no other verdict than what we gave last night; we have no other verdict to give."

Another of the justices, Sir Thomas Bludworth, commented gloomily: "I knew Mr. Bushell would not yield," and the Recorder threatened again: "I will have a positive verdict, or you will starve for it." After the night they had just spent, the jury could not look on this as an empty threat.

Penn desired to ask one question: Did the court accept the verdict "Not guilty," given of William Mead?

"It cannot be a verdict," said the Recorder, "because you are indicted for a conspiracy; and one being found guilty and not the other, it could not be a verdict."

Penn's answer was quick. "If not guilty be not a verdict, then you make of the jury and Magna Carta a mere nose of wax. . . . And if William Mead be not guilty, it consequently follows that I am clear, since you have indicted us of a conspiracy, and I could not possibly conspire alone."

But for the third time the verdict was rejected and the jury sent back to find another. Again it returned with the one answer it had to give.

The court was well-nigh beside itself with rage. It threatened to set a mark on Edward Bushell, to have an eye on him, to cut his nose. And now Penn's voice rings out:

"It is intolerable that my jury should be thus menaced. Is this according to the fundamental law? Are they not my proper judges by the great charter of England? What hope is there of ever having justice done, when juries are threatened and their verdicts rejected? I am concerned to speak and grieved to see such arbitrary proceedings. Did not the Lieutenant of the Tower render one of them worse than a felon? And do you not plainly seem to condemn such for factious fellows who answer not your ends? Unhappy are those juries who are threatened to be fined and starved and ruined if they give not in their verdicts contrary to their consciences."

The Recorder had nothing to say in answer but: "My lord, you must take a course with that fellow."

"Jailer, bring fetters," commanded the Chief Justice, "and stake him to the ground."

"Do your pleasure," replied Penn superbly, "I matter not your fetters."

And now the Recorder's rage did what Penn was later to tell his children anger always does: it threw him into a desperate inconvenience. He made a speech that echoed around London and that he bitterly regretted afterwards.

"Till now," he said, "I never understood the reason of the policy and prudence of the Spaniards in suffering the Inquisition among them. And certainly it will never be well with us till something like the Spanish Inquisition be in England."

It was a dreadful thing to say. The torture and terror of the Spanish Inquisition were fresh in men's minds— Penn's grandfather, Giles Penn, had suffered from it—and in England Popery was more feared and detested than non-conformity.

For the fourth time the jury was ordered to go find another verdict; this time they refused to go, saying there was no other verdict. The Recorder in a passion left the bench, sputtering: "I protest I will sit here no longer to hear these things," but the Mayor called to him to stay while he uttered a few more threats, had the sheriff take the jury up to their room, and adjourned the court.

The prisoners were sent back to Newgate, where at least they had more freedom and comfort than the jury.

At seven o'clock on the morning of Monday, September fifth, the court sat again. The jury staggered in, wan, white, hungry, thirsty, and disheveled.

"Look upon the prisoners," said the Clerk. "What say you, is William Penn guilty or not guilty?"

"Not guilty."

"What say you? Is William Mead guilty, or not guilty?"

"Not guilty."

It was plain and definite this time. There was nothing the Bench could do except to call the roll and make each juror give his verdict separately. Everyone answered firmly: "Not guilty."

The people in the galleries were pleased, so pleased

that they "made a kind of hymn about it." All over the courtroom there were little murmurs of satisfaction.

But the affair was not over. The Recorder had his last word. "I am sorry, gentlemen, you have followed your own judgments and opinions rather than the good and wholesome advice which was given you. God keep my life out of your hands: but for this the court fines you forty marks a man, and imprisonment till paid."

They had been threatened with fines and imprisonment, they had faced the ugly temper of the Bench, they must have known this was coming. But forty marks was a lot of money, about twenty-six pounds sterling, in a day when a lieutenant in the Plymouth colony, for instance, got an annual salary of twenty marks, and women worked in the hayfields for a penny a day.

Penn then stepped up toward the Bench and demanded his liberty. He was told that he too was in for fines—the forty mark fine imposed at the beginning of the session for wearing his hat. He began to quote the Magna Carta again, but the Recorder had had all he could stand. "Take him away," he implored, "take him away, take him out of the court."

But before he went young William Penn had one thing more to say. He said it. "I can never urge the fundamental laws of England but you cry: 'Take him away, take him away.' But it is no wonder, since the Spanish Inquisition hath so great a place in the Recorder's heart. God Almighty, who is just, will judge you for these things."

So the prisoners who had been acquitted, and the jury who had acquitted them, went together to Newgate prison.

That night Penn wrote to his father. "Because I cannot come, I write." He told him the story of the trial, ending: "I am more concerned at thy distemper and the pains that attend it, than at my own mere imprisonment, which works for the best."

The next day he wrote: "I entreat thee not to purchase my liberty. They will repent them of their proceedings. I am now a prisoner notoriously against law."

And the next: "I am persuaded some clearer way will suddenly be found to obtain my liberty, which is no way so desirable to me as on the account of being with thee. ... My present restraint is so far from being humor that I would rather perish than release myself by so indirect a course as to satiate their revengeful, avaricious appetites. The advantage of such freedom would fall very far short of the trouble of accepting it."

To pay the fine would be to admit its justice. What he wanted was either to be released by the court, or to bring suit against the judges for illegal imprisonment. In this way a principle could be established. This was the course the jury was taking. Every six hours they demanded their freedom, and when at length they were released on bail, they brought suit against the judges—and won their case. The whole body of judges in the King's Bench Court decided that no jury could be fined for its verdict. So it was that as a result of the trial of William

Penn the sacredness of trial by jury was established for all time.

But that was nearly a year later.

The Admiral could not wait. He was dying, and he wanted to see his beloved son William again. He secretly paid his fine, and Mead's too, and they were set free.

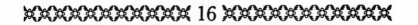

16

The Admiral's Last Anchorage

"SON WILLIAM, I am weary of the world! I would not live over my days again if I could command them with a wish."

The Admiral's forty-nine years had been full of battle and of strife; none of it he regretted so much as the struggle against his own son. Wholeheartedly now he recognized and respected the courage and steadfastness of the tall young man whom he loved more than anything in the world. Recognizing too that Son William was likely always to be in need of someone to protect him from the dangers his religion would expose him to, Sir William turned to the most powerful of his own friends. To the Duke of York he sent a message, asking of him as a dying request that he would protect his son so far as he could and use his influence with the King on William's behalf. The answer came back with heartening promptness; both the Duke and the King gave their promise.

Six days the Admiral and William had together after William returned from Newgate to Wanstead. The father had three pieces of advice to give the son:

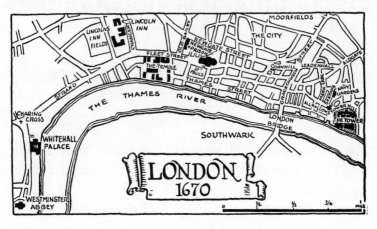

"First, let nothing in this world tempt you to wrong your conscience; so you will keep peace at home, which will be a feast to you in the day of trouble. Secondly, whatever you design to do, lay it justly and time it seasonably, for that gives security and dispatch. Lastly, be not troubled at disappointments, for if they may be recovered, do it; if they cannot, trouble is vain."

And later he said: "Live in love."

He died on the sixteenth of September.

He was buried, as he had asked, beside his mother in the church of St. Mary Redcliffe in Bristol, the beautiful church which Queen Elizabeth had called "the fairest and goodliest parish church in all England." Three or four companies of foot-soldiers headed the funeral procession; the armor he had worn on the *Royal Charles* was carried for all to see; the hearse was drawn by six horses and above it waved three flags representing the three squadrons which he had commanded. All Bristol turned out to do honor to its famous son; all over England people recalled the part that Admiral Penn had played in her naval triumphs; and the King and the Duke of York remembered that they had given him a promise.

Lovingly, his son wrote his epitaph, which finished with these words:

"He withdrew, prepared and made for his end; and with a gentle and even gale, in much peace, arrived and anchored in his last and best port, at Wanstead in the County of Essex, the 16th of September, 1670, being then but forty-nine and four months old. To his name and memory his surviving lady hath erected this remembrance."

It was the end of an era for young William Penn. His trial trip was over. His Admiral was gone. He was himself commander now, and the great voyage of his life lay before him.

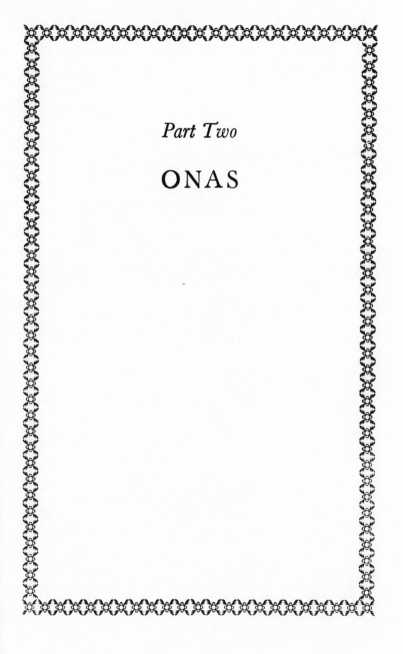

Part Two

ONAS

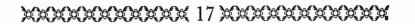

17

William and Gulielma

IT WAS never William Penn's way to sit down with
grief. Instead, he turned sorrow into action. When
his heart ached for his father, whom he missed sorely, he
plunged deeper than ever into work.

Much of that work was writing. His pen scratched
furiously over sheet after sheet of paper. He wrote
letters. He wrote an account of the trial in order to tell
people what had happened and to rouse them to the
principles of liberty involved in it. He wrote pamphlets
and tracts. The Society of Friends was being attacked on
all sides, and William Penn, who was university-trained
and who had studied theology at Saumur, was just the
person to write its defense. He had the knowledge, he
had the conviction, the fighting spirit—and the words.
Strong, pointed, colorful words were needed. People did
not mince matters in those days, least of all religious
matters.

When the authorities at Oxford encouraged the students to "rag" the Quakers cruelly, and sent spies among
the Non-Conformists to make friends with them and then
imprisoned and fined and whipped them for the things
the spies reported, William Penn wrote a hot letter to

the Vice-Chancellor. "Poor Mushroom, wilt thou war against the Lord? . . . Repent of thy proud, peevish, and bitter actings." (The Mushroom made no answer and, so far as anyone knows, did little repenting.)

When a Baptist minister in West Wycombe named Ives preached a sermon against the Quakers, William Penn challenged him to a public debate. They had a somewhat stormy time of it, but when it was over Thomas Ellwood, who went with Penn, celebrated his victory with a song of triumph:

> *"Truth hath prevailed; the Enemies did fly;*
> *We are in Safety; Praise to God on high."*

The other side also claimed to have won the victory, so that everyone was satisfied.

Late in the fall William went into Buckinghamshire, where he stayed with his distant cousins in their manor house outside the little village of Penn. There in the deep country quiet he went on with his writing. The air was fresh and cold and smelled of damp leaves and wood-smoke; there were only the occasional country noises, rooks cawing in the leafless woods, the frosty sound of wood-chopping, the neighing of a horse, the creak of wagon wheels in deep-rutted lanes. And indoors all was warmth and comfort, firelight gleaming on polished silver and old oak, a desk to write where no one interrupted, and pleasant talk about the dinner table. The Penns of Penn were not Quakers, but they were cordial and sympathetic to their handsome young Quaker cousin.

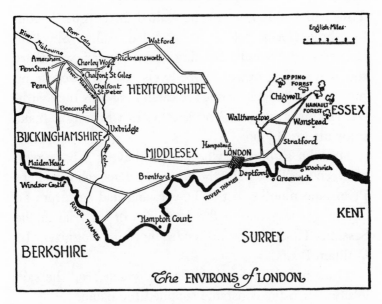

The ENVIRONS of LONDON

It was an ideal place to write. Better still, it was close to Amersham and Guli Springett.

It was a happy time—but going up to London one Sunday to meeting ended it. It was the Wheeler Street meeting this time, and the day was February 5, 1671, just five months since the jury acquitted Penn of the charge of speaking to an unlawful assembly in Grace-church Street. The Mayor and the Lord Lieutenant of the Tower had not forgiven him; they had been biding their time, and once again soldiers came to a Friends' meeting with a warrant made out in advance for William Penn.

They seized him as soon as he began to speak and took him and another man, Thomas Rudyard, with him, to the

Tower of London, where he waited in the guard room for three hours before he was led before Sir John Robinson. Sir Samuel Starling, Lord Mayor, was there too, and several others. Nobody else was allowed in, no jury, for the judges planned to catch Penn this time without risking a jury, and no spectators who might make sympathetic "hymns."

Sir John Robinson, who used to have a private path between the Tower and the Navy Gardens, who had kept Penn nine months in the Tower, and had seen him all day long every one of the four days of his trial at the Sessions House, now pretended not to recognize Mr. William Penn.

"I do not desire to know such as you are," he said loftily, when the constable supplied the name.

"If not," said Penn reasonably, "why didst thou send for me hither?"

Sir John was slow to learn that he always came off badly in a battle of wits with William Penn. He expected prisoners to be frightened and silent before him, not to come forth with quick and apt retorts. In his buffle-headed way he floundered now into a legal discussion during which the prisoner proved that neither the Conventicle Act nor the Oxford Act applied to him in this case. But there was still another way to get him, and Sir John Robinson and Sir Samuel Starling were ready with it. The Lieutenant of the Tower produced the oath of allegiance, and told Penn he must swear, knowing very well that Quakers could not take an oath of any kind. Penn refused, declaring at the same time his loyalty to the King.

"Well," pronounced Sir John with a show of reluctance, "I must send you to Newgate for six months, and when they are expired, you will come out."

"Is that all?" said Penn. "Thou well knowest a larger imprisonment has not daunted me. . . . I would have thee and all other men to know that I scorn that religion which is not worth suffering for, and able to sustain those that are afflicted for it. Mine is."

"Send a corporal with a file of musketeers along with him."

"No, no, send thy lackey. I know the way to Newgate."

Well indeed he knew the way to Newgate and he knew what Newgate was like. Six months of it. And Guli in Amersham.

At first he and Rudyard hired a room in the Master's side, hoping thus to have more privacy, but they found the jailer so grasping and abusive that in protest they went over to the common side. There in all the crowds, the dirt, the smells, the noise, Penn wrote harder than ever.

A man who signed himself S.S. had answered his pamphlet on the trial with a scandalous attack on Admiral Penn, accusing him of cowardice in failing to take Hispaniola and of stealing from the prizes which his ships captured for the King. Nothing ever hurt or angered William Penn more than unjust charges against

his father. He had the gold chain and medal which Cromwell had given the Admiral, and he had still the pride
and hero-worship which swelled his small boy heart
when he heard his father's name read out in the Thanksgiving service. Though as a Quaker he could not approve
of fighting, as a son he took his pen in hand to say with
all his power that his father had been a brave and true—
and successful—fighter. As for the Admiral's honesty,
vividly William remembered how a captured ship had
been brought in with great chests of Spanish gold upon
her; how his mother, longing for one of the strange coins
for a keepsake, had offered to pay its equivalent in English money for it; and how his father had refused to let
her have it. It was the King's, he had said, and it must go
to the King exactly as he got it. He never "took or
caused to be taken one clove, nutmeg, blade of mace, or
skein of silk." And they said such a man was dishonest!
He called his answer "Truth Rescued from Imposture."
At the end, remembering his Friendly principles of love
and forgiveness, he relented so far toward S.S. (who
might have been Samuel Starling) as to write: "I wish
him repentance of these impieties and sincerely declare
my hearty forgiveness of all his aggravating injuries."

When at length, early in August, he came out of
prison, the London yearly meeting was just over, and
Friends were still there from all the countryside. They
were full of great news. George Fox was going to
America! It was upon him from the Lord to go across the
seas and visit the plantations there, and eleven Friends

were going with him. They would be away a year or more.

Margaret, his wife, only recently released from prison in Lancaster Castle, was there to say farewell to him. Mary Penington was there, and Guli with her. They and some other Friends were going to Gravesend with George Fox to see him off. Would William go too?

Out of the deathly murkiness of Newgate into such life and sunshine as this! William Penn's heart sang.

Early on the morning of August 12 they left James Strutts's house in Wapping and boarded one of the King's barges: George and Margaret Fox, Mary Penington, Guli Springett, and William Penn. It was a deeply happy group; two so recently out of prison that the very air was new and delicious, the sunshine heavenly, and the river and the houses along its banks miraculously beautiful; four loving hearts re-united; a high and holy adventure lying before one of them.

The barge slipped down the river among the other boats, the fishing smacks and wherries, the frigates and lighters and barges. Past Deptford where the royal ship-yards were, past Greenwich and its hospital, past the Essex marshes where the sun shone over level stretches of bright green, and water birds rose out of the reeds and soared up into the blue of the sky. Now and then a cloud passed overhead and in its shadow they were cool for a little while.

William was pale and thin, Guli thought, but more handsome than ever. He was alive throughout all his

long length, strong and eager, and yet gentle. She found
the combination of his Friendly simplicity and the un-
conscious elegance which he would never lose completely
fascinating—and she wondered if it was right to notice
such things. He was so modest, too, about all he had
done and suffered, so loving and deferential with George
Fox. Dear George Fox. She looked over at him and
found his piercing yet tender gaze upon her. She hoped
he would not encounter too many dangers and hardships
in America. But then, there were dangers for Friends
everywhere. Hardly one of them had not been more than
once in prison: Margaret Fox; and George Fox, her
own step-father (so many times); and William. . . .

William thought that Guli was more beautiful than
ever, because the loveliness of her spirit shone in her
face. He thought of their home together; they must not
delay much longer now. Somewhere in Buckinghamshire, not far from Amersham, so that Guli need not be
separated from her mother. He wondered why her eyes
looked, just for a moment, sad. He would change that;
he would make her happy all the time. . . .

They were passing Gravesend. The slanting rays of
the sun turned to gold the windows of the houses along
the shore. The river had widened out and it was full of
ships riding at anchor. William felt his pulses quicken.
Ships. They made him think of his father.

Three miles below the town they found the ketch
called the *Industry* and George Fox went aboard. The

rest returned to Gravesend to spend the night in lodgings.

They found the other Friends already there, the eleven who were to go to America and those who had come with them to see them off. Everything was bustle and stir. Somebody's sea-chest was missing. Everybody was relieved to know that George Fox had come from London and was on the boat. Suppose he had been arrested and put in prison at the last minute! Some thought it would be a good thing to have a meeting for worship before supper, and others wanted to have supper first. A woman who was not going turned aside to hide the tears that welled up in her eyes. America so far, and full of unknown terrors—and what would John get to eat! A woman who was going tried to be calm and subdue her joy; she felt she was directly chosen of the Lord for a great work.

Then in the midst of it all John Hull arrived. He was a youngish man, rather recently convinced. He had waited on the Lord in his room that morning, he explained, and at the end of two hours he had been moved to follow them in order to go on the voyage to America with them. So at ten o'clock he had left London, and here he was. He was pale with the suddenness of his decision, but very determined.

It was all immensely stirring. Those who were not going looked at John Hull with wonder and a kind of longing.

Early the next morning before it was light George Pattison roused up everyone. Through the morning mist they went in barges to the *Industry*, which had already weighed anchor and was ready to sail.

Now that the moment had come, everyone was very quiet. Hearts were full. They had but a little time for a leave-taking filled with tenderness and courage.

In the sunrise at the turn of the tide, one after another of the ships in the river slipped away, frigates, merchantmen, fishing-boats, and the little ketch *Industry*. They watched her growing smaller in the opalescent light until between the mist and water they could see her no longer.

"I had an opening of joy as to America," said William Penn slowly, "ten years ago at Oxford."

Guli touched his arm, and he turned back to her.

But it stayed in his mind that George Fox and twelve others had gone to America, and he—what had he done? Been in prison—but so had everyone else. Written pamphlets. What was writing? And now he was going to marry the love of his heart and settle down to the life of a well-to-do country gentleman. No hardship there, no struggle, no danger.

His conscience would not let him rest. Quakerism, spreading slowly through Holland and seeping into Germany, was meeting persecution there. Off went Penn to Holland, taking Thomas Rudyard, his late companion in Newgate, with him. He never said very much about that trip afterwards, except that it was through "a very dark country" and "under a great weight and suffering in my spirit," and by the end of October he was back again in England.

He took lodgings at Walthamstow, where he could often see his mother at Wanstead, and from where he could explore the country in search of a home for Guli and himself. He found it at last, Basing House at Rickmansworth, a comfortable and pleasant dwelling with a garden and great lime trees, near Amersham, and not too far from either London or Walthamstow.

They both declared their intention, as the Friendly way was, to their separate monthly meetings, and after it had been approved, a special meeting was appointed for their marriage at King's Farm, in Chorley Wood.

The old farm house, timbered in the Elizabethan way, sat on the top of a hill overlooking Rickmansworth. On April 4, 1672, nearly fifty people gathered in the beamed parlor to see William Penn and Gulielma Springett married. Lady Penn was there, and Dick, who was now a tall stripling, none too strong; Pegg in Yorkshire was too far away to come. Isaac and Mary Penington were there, and Mary and John, their children; Guli's aunt, Elizabeth Springett, from Surrey; Thomas Ellwood and his wife Mary, from their place near Amersham; George Whitehead from London; and many others from the neighborhood.

In the silence they sat together, while the April breeze stirred the tree shadows outside, a blackbird sang, and the April sun came in through the casement windows to shine on the oak gateleg table where the certificate lay waiting to be signed, on a jug of daffodils still cold with dew, and touched the golden hair of the bride, the broad shoulders of the groom.

They stood up. Solemnly William took Guli's hand in his—and how small and fragile and white it was in his strong one!—and said: "In the presence of God and these our friends, I, William, take thee, Gulielma, to be my wife, promising to be to thee loving, kind, and faithful so long as it shall please God to continue our natural lives."

And then she in her turn took his hand and promised to be to him loving, kind, and faithful.

And so they were married. Ten years later he was to write to her: "God knows, and thou knowest it, I can say it was a match of Providence's own making."

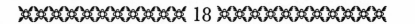

18

Some Beginnings

BRISTOL FAIR, which had been held in St. James's churchyard every year in July since the twelfth century, was the greatest fair in England. Here merchants from all over the country brought their wares: woolens and leather goods of all kinds, linens, farming tools, and all the things that women love, ornaments and trinkets and toys for the children. Here came people from near and far to do their shopping for a whole year, and see the world, and have a good time.

Here, in July 1673, Quakers came flocking, for George Fox was just back from America.

The Penns came too. They had been on a "journey in the ministry" through the west country, attending meetings and preaching—William, that is, not Guli—and they finished their trip with a week or so at Bristol. It had been a happy year for them, save for one sorrow. Their baby, their little Gulielma, had lived only two months. For the rest, it had been a time of content and ever-deepening love at home, and of peace abroad. The King had issued a Declaration of Indulgence, setting aside the laws made by Parliament against the Non-Conformists, and for a little while persecution took a holiday. It did not last long, for Parliament, getting the upper hand in the endless struggle for power, forced the King to withdraw it, but at least there had been a breathing space, and many Friends had been released from prison.

In Bristol Friends were enjoying their new meeting-house, which had been built on the foundations of an ancient Dominican Friary. To one side of it the old orchard of the friars stretched away to the open country; in front a branch of the river Frome flowed past, and beyond that were the walls of ruined Bristol Castle, and the town itself rising on the hill above. Here, stirred and illumined by the presence of George Fox, they held "many and glorious meetings" this July. And after the meetings, walking through the orchard or sitting in the sunshine in Dennis Hollister's garden in the Broad Mead, William and Guli listened to Fox's tales of his journey to America and his descriptions of the country he found there.

From Carolina to Rhode Island and back again to Virginia he had made his difficult way with his little band of Friends, sleeping at night in the woods beside a fire, or in an Indian wigwam or a settler's log cabin. Some Friends there were in Virginia, where the Episcopal Church was established as in England, more in Lord Baltimore's Roman Catholic colony of Maryland, some few in New England, though the Puritans persecuted them there. What had interested him more was that great stretch of almost uninhabited land between Maryland and Connecticut. He had crossed the Delaware at the Dutch village of New Castle, and then for days, with an Indian guide, he had ridden through forest and bogs so lonely that sometimes for a whole day at a time he would not see a soul, white man or Indian, or any sign of human habitation. At Middletown, which was a sea-coast town with frame houses and streets, he got a boat to put him over on Long Island, where there were three settlements, and Quakers in all of them. But between New Castle and Middletown—nothing.

So George Fox talked and William Penn listened, and their unspoken thoughts marched together. All that un-inhabited land—and Friends oppressed in England, per-secuted, forbidden to worship God according to their consciences.

The Duke of York had taken the land from the Dutch in 1664. The part of it on the west bank of the Delaware he had kept, but that on the east he had granted to Lord Berkeley and Sir George Carteret, who had called it New Jersey, because Carteret was born on the island of Jersey. Only recently Lord Berkeley had decided to sell his share and was waiting for a buyer.

And if Friends should buy it?

They talked about it at Bristol, and the next month at Rickmansworth when George and Margaret Fox and some other Friends came to visit the Penns at Basing House.

There were many things to consider. The Parliament, having forced the King to withdraw the Declaration of

Indulgence, now passed a Test Act which provided that no one could hold office under the Crown unless he would receive the sacrament according to the rites of the Church of England, which excluded the Catholics and all kinds of Protestant Non-Conformists. Another wave of persecution was curving to break.

Could they prepare for Friends a refuge beyond the seas? After much consideration it was decided that a Friend named Edward Byllynge should buy Lord Berkeley's share of New Jersey for a thousand pounds, and another Friend, named John Fenwick, was to be his agent. When this was all settled, William Penn turned his mind to other things.

He was soon drawn into the affair in a way he did not expect. Edward Byllynge and John Fenwick quarreled, and Penn was called upon to arbitrate between them. It was a great compliment to a young man not yet thirty to ask him to settle such a difference between two men much older than himself, but it was not an easy task he had to do. After much thought he made what he considered a fair decision—and then to his grief John Fenwick refused to accept it. More letters, interviews, reasonings. At length Fenwick declared himself satisfied, and departed in the *Griffith* with his family and some others, the first English ship ever to sail up the Delaware. They landed at a "pleasant rich spot," and called it Salem, city of peace.

But that was not all. Edward Byllynge was not able

after all to pay for his share. He wished to make it over to his creditors, and they, looking about for someone to act as trustee for them, decided on William Penn and two other Friends to help him. And now indeed he had his hands full. This land had to be separated from that of Sir George Carteret, and after many negotiations it was agreed between them that New Jersey should be divided into two parts: East Jersey belonging to Sir George Carteret, and West Jersey belonging to the Quakers.

The territory of West Jersey must be divided into a hundred parts, ten of them reserved to Fenwick, and the other ninety sold for the creditors. Some kind of concessions and agreements must be drawn up that would serve as a constitution for the settlers to live by. And who was to do that? Who had been doing all the work? William Penn.

Very well. First and foremost, there should be religious liberty. An assembly elected by the people. Trial by jury.

The deeper he got into the business, the more interested he became. And the more he came to feel that this was not the way he would like to do it. It had come about in too helter-skelter a way. He remembered what his father had said: "Whatever you design to do, lay it justly and time it seasonably." This had come too hastily and too soon, before the right plans were worked out. But he did his best. He reread those books he had read at Oxford, More's *Utopia*, and Harrington's *Oceana;* he studied the Puritan constitutions of the New England colonies. But all the time he felt as if what he was doing were only a sort of preparatory exercise.

In 1677 and 1678 five more ships sailed for West Jersey, with eight hundred emigrants, and they founded a town which they called Burlington. Though the land had been bought from Lord Berkeley, they followed the example of the earlier Dutch settlers on the other side of the river and bought it again from the Indians, who were after all the real owners. A strange enough assortment of things they paid for it: looking glasses and guns, scissors and red paint and jew's harps—and rum. But the rum was a mistake. That must be changed. It was bad for the Indians.

Meanwhile the wave of persecution had broken, and once again the Quakers were engulfed. George Fox was one of the first to be arrested. When the magistrates offered him the oath of allegiance and he—of course—refused it, they clapped him into Worcester Castle.

Penn did his best to get him out. As soon as he heard about it, he went to London to confer with Friends, and they came to the conclusion that the best thing was to exert any influence at court that they could scrape up to have him freed. William Penn and William Mead were chosen to go on this errand.

It was five years since Penn had been to court, and he had been in prison three times in those years; he was not sure how he would be received.

Rather cautiously he went about it, going first to the

Earl of Middlesex, who advised him not to apply directly to the King, but to the Duke of York. He himself, he promised, would arrange it—and very elaborate his arrangements were. He arranged for a gentleman named Fleetwood Shepherd to arrange with the secretary of the Duchess of York for them to see the Duke. When the appointed day actually came, however, there was such a crowd of people at the Duke's palace, that even the Duchess's secretary himself could not get into the royal presence.

While they were hesitating in the drawing-room, wondering what to do, Colonel Aston, gentleman in waiting, who had known the Admiral, recognized Penn. After that all was easy. Rather as King Charles had done, years before, the Duke popped out of his room to greet William Penn cordially. His manner, however, was not superficial and gay, like Charles's; it was simple, serious, sincere.

He read the petition that the two Quakers had brought with them, and after a moment said:

"Gentlemen, I am against all persecution for the sake of religion. I am for doing to others as I would have others do unto me; and I think it would be happy for the world if all were of that mind—for I am sure," he added, a faint smile lightening his narrow, pallid face, "that no man is willing to be persecuted himself for his own conscience. As for the Quakers, I look upon you as a quiet industrious people, and though I am not of your belief, yet I like your good lives."

He promised that he would speak to his brother the King in George Fox's behalf. Then, having disposed of their business, he turned with particular courtesy to William Penn.

"I well remember how your father and I served together in the Navy, and my promise to him that I would have a care for you in all regards. I wonder you have not been here before. When you have business here, come, and I will give orders that you have access to me."

With that, graciously, he withdrew. Penn and Mead, in the awed silence of hopes more than fulfilled, left the house, and not till they were outside in the garden did Mead find words to express, over and over, his wonder and joy at the Duke's kindness and condescension.

For William Penn it was the renewing of a genuine friendship. The Duke's words about religious liberty warmed his heart and filled him with hope for the future. He liked the Duke, and as always when he liked anyone, he trusted him wholly.

The Duke did indeed prevail upon the King to sign a release for George Fox, but it "stuck with the Lord Keeper," who stubbornly delayed acting on it, so that it was actually more than a year before George Fox was set free.

At home William and Guli were going through deep waters. Twins had been born to them, a girl and a boy, whom they named Mary and William, but like their first baby these little ones also died, the boy at three months and the girl at thirteen months. Their hearts

torn, they sought distractedly a reason for these re-
peated tragedies. Perhaps Rickmansworth was unhealthy.
Perhaps the constant stream of visitors who stopped
there on their way to and from London was bad for
children. Basing House was sad for them now—how
could it be otherwise?—in spite of the shining happiness
that they first brought to it. There was Dick too, eight-
een-year-old Dick, so winning and so delicate, who came
to visit them, and like the babies, slipped away from
them like an unmoored boat in an outgoing tide.

Suddenly able to endure the place no longer, they
packed up and moved to Walthamstow, so that their
fourth child, Springett, might be born away from Rickmansworth. But Walthamstow was only a temporary
lodging. Penn began at once to look about for a perma-
nent home for them.

In Sussex, near where Mary Penington had grown
up, he found an estate called Worminghurst. It lay on
the crest of a ridge, open to the sun and to the wind that
came from the sea beyond the South Downs on one side,
or across the farm-patterned sweep of the Sussex Weald
on the other. The long, substantial, generous-looking
brick house, with its roof of Horsham stone, was shaded
by a group of great Spanish chestnut trees, and below its
terraces and gardens a little lake reflected the sky and
the moving clouds.

Here, to this happy place, Penn brought his little
family, Gulielma, the love of his heart, and Springett, his
son.

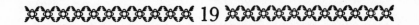

19

By Boat and Wagon

"**B**EING the first day of the week," wrote Penn in his journal, "I left my dear wife and family at Worminghurst in Sussex, in the fear and love of God, and came well to London that night."

When they were first married, Guli went on all his preaching journeys with him, through the home counties of Kent and Surrey and Essex, or west into Somerset and Wiltshire, but now it seemed best for her not to leave Worminghurst and Springett, who was a year and a half old. This was, moreover, going to be a strenuous and difficult trip, and Guli Penn was not strong.

So William kissed her, and rode away through Sussex. His heart, heavy at first with the pain of parting, grew lighter as he rode on, and by the time he reached the North Downs, he was filled with zest and enthusiasm for the adventure that beckoned ahead. It was always William Penn's way to look hopefully forward, never backward, and before him now lay Holland and Germany. He was going this time, not hesitatingly as he had gone six years before, with a single companion even more uncertain than he was, but confidently, with George Fox himself (dear George Fox, as all who knew him well in-

164

variably spoke of him) and seven others. They were planning to visit some Friends' meetings that had sprung up in Holland, to organize a yearly meeting for Europe, and to venture at least a little way into Germany.

The first night on his way William Penn spent in London, the second with his mother at Wanstead, the third in Colchester. The following day, which was the twenty-fifth of July, he reached Harwich in time for dinner.

He found his companions all there before him: dear George Fox and his step-daughter Isabel Yeamans, who was going along to take care of him, for his fourteen months in Worcester Castle had done his health no good; George Keith, a young Scotsman who was mathematician at Aberdeen University, and his wife Elizabeth, and another brilliant young Scot, Robert Barclay of Ury, who in background and point of view was more like William Penn than any of the other Quakers of his time. Four years younger than Penn, he too came from a family of wealth and position—through his mother he was third cousin to the King. He too had been more than once in prison, and had written a great Quaker book, his *Apology*, which he had published first in Latin and was now translating into English; he too coming on this trip had left a young wife and little son behind him. Unlike William Penn, however, he had not had to battle against his father for his right to his belief; in fact Colonel David Barclay had been convinced first, and Robert had followed his father into Quakerism. Three other Friends were of the party, George Watts, John Furley of Colchester, and William Tallcoatt, all older men.

They went aboard the packet-boat in the late July twilight; the master of the line, having served under Admiral Penn, made a great point of seeing to it that they had the best accommodations in the ship. At three o'clock on Thursday morning they sailed, and late on Friday evening they came into sight of Brielle. There, half a league from shore, the ship dropped anchor and proposed to spend the night.

William Penn and Robert Barclay could not stand it! What, spend the night rocking at anchor in the North Sea when they might be on Dutch soil, perhaps getting their work started at once! Besides, Friends were coming from Rotterdam to meet them there. They hunted up the captain and made their own arrangements.

Two of the sailors let down a little boat from the side of the ship and rowed them to shore. Triumphantly they approached the city—and found the gate closed for the night. No amount of shouting and knocking roused the gate-keeper. There were no houses outside the wall, the little boat had gone back to the ship, and there they were, at night, in a strange country. Somewhat ruefully, they climbed into a fishing-boat moored to the wharf, and spent the night in hunched and chilly discomfort.

The next morning as soon as the gate was opened, they went into the city, where almost at once they bumped into some Dutch Friends who had come with boats to meet the English Quakers and take them to

Rotterdam. Among them was Benjamin Furley, whom
Penn had met in Rotterdam when he was there before;
he was the son of John Furley of Colchester, and a friend
of Algernon Sidney and John Locke; and he had a famous library.

After that all went smoothly. They visited Rotterdam
and held meetings there, and then went on to Amsterdam, where they stayed nearly a week.

On Monday August 6, George Keith, Robert Barclay,
Benjamin Furley, and William Penn set forth on a trip
into Germany. They were a congenial quartet, all fairly
near the same age, all enthusiastic, all keen on books and
writing. They took a number of Quaker pamphlets with
them which they gave to people who showed any
interest; they preached in almost every village and town
they came to, they traveled by boat along the rivers and
by post-wagon across country, in all kinds of weather.
They were often uncomfortable and still more often
weary, but they paid no more attention to their own
chilled and aching bodies than they paid to the beauty of
the land through which they went. It was souls they were
interested in. They found a "breathing, hungering, seeking people scattered up and down this great land of
Germany," with whom they made untiring efforts to
share the truth that was life to them.

In the northeast part of Westphalia, they came upon a
little town with seven church spires. Here lived Princess
Elizabeth Palatine of the Rhine. She was a gracious and
stately woman of sixty, first cousin of King Charles II of

England, and she might have been Queen of Poland if she had been willing to become a Catholic. In her younger days, she had been a favorite pupil of the great French philosopher Descartes; now she was abbess of the Protestant foundation of Herwerden, interested in Quakerism and eager to know more about it. Robert Barclay was a distant cousin of hers and he had visited her the year before; Benjamin Furley she also knew, William Penn she had corresponded with. She welcomed them all cordially, and they spent four deeply stirring days in Herwerden.

They stayed at the inn in the village, and went twice a day to the Princess's house to talk with her and the Countess de Hornes, her companion, and to hold meetings with them and with the people of the neighborhood. On their last day there, the Princess, taking Penn by the hand, tried to tell him something of what his words had meant to her, but she could not. Turning away toward the window so that he could not see her face, she said brokenly: "I cannot speak to you; my heart is full." And as he was leaving, she begged him: "Will you not come hither again? Pray, call here as you return out of Germany."

The next morning at seven the quartet broke up. Robert Barclay started on his way back to Amsterdam, and ultimately to Scotland, and the other three set forth toward Frankfurt, two hundred miles away. The weather was wet and the roads deep in mud. It took them a week to make the journey.

From Frankfurt they sailed to Mainz and up the Rhine to Crisheim, where to their joy they found a meeting already established. "There is a lovely, sweet, and true sense among them," wrote Penn in his journal. "We were greatly comforted in them and they in us. Poor hearts! a little handful, surrounded with great and mighty countries of darkness." They stayed three days with the Friends in Crisheim, and left them reluctantly.

Less than a week after this happy experience the one fiasco of the whole journey befell them.

From Crisheim they sailed down the Rhine again, stopping along the way at towns where they had been told there were Seekers, until they came to the city of Duisburg. There they hoped to meet the Countess of Falchenstein and Bruch, who they had heard was a remarkable young woman, religiously inclined and interested in Quakerism. They asked a Dr. Mastricht, to whom they had a letter of introduction, to help them get in touch with her.

Seeing the Countess proved, however, to be a delicate and difficult matter, for her stern father, who had no patience at all with queer religions, kept a strict watch over her. "However," said Dr. Mastricht, "the fittest time is the present; for you may find her at the minister's house in Mülheim across the river from her father's castle. She spends every Sunday there."

It was already well along in the afternoon, but the good doctor gave them a letter to the Countess and showed them the way to Mülheim. The path went six miles through a wood, and then wound behind the Count's castle and orchard.

As luck would have it, at the very instant they passed by the castle, the Count came out to walk. Seeing the strangers, he sent his attendant to ask who they were, where they came from, and where they were going. Then, not waiting for the man to bring back their answers, he beckoned them to him and put his questions to them himself.

"We are Englishmen," replied Penn, "come from Holland, and we are going no farther in these parts than thy own town of Mülheim."

One of the Count's gentlemen hinted: "Do you know whom you're talking to? Don't you usually behave rather differently before noblemen and in the presence of princes?"

Hat-honor again. Penn said courteously: "We are not conscious ourselves of any disrespect or unseemly behavior."

"Then why don't you pull off your hats?" said another gentleman sharply. "Is it respect to stand covered in the presence of the sovereign of the country?"

"It is our practice in the presence of our own sovereign, who is a great king," Penn explained. "We uncover to nobody but to God."

"Quakers!" exclaimed the Count in horror, as if he had seen a poisonous snake. "We want no Quakers here! Get off my land. You shall not go into my town."

They did their best to tell him that they were a peaceable people, that they respected him and would gladly do him any real service, but he would not listen. He called up his soldiers, and ordered them to see the Quakers off his land immediately.

They had to go. But unwilling to be completely routed, they expounded the principles of Quakerism to their military escort as they went, and the soldiers, better mannered than their master, "were civil."

The six miles back to Duisburg seemed long. The wood, cheerful enough earlier in the day, now was "tedious and solitary," and however much they tried to comfort themselves by reminding each other of pious men of long ago who had wandered up and down like poor pilgrims and strangers on the earth, they felt a little depressed; particularly Penn, who, however much rudeness he had suffered from the magistrates, had never before been forcibly put off anybody's land before he had a chance to say a word.

Between nine and ten they reached the walls of Duisburg—and found the gates shut. There was nothing to do but to make the best of it and lie down in the field outside. About three o'clock, when the first faint morning lights and noises were beginning to appear, they got up and walked about to stretch their cramped bodies, until, soon after the clock in the town hall struck five—welcome sound in the silent and empty fields—the city gates were opened.

Later that day Penn, distressed at the thought of the Countess, who was not getting the spiritual food she craved, wrote her an inspiring and comforting letter. And then, having still something on his mind, he trimmed his pen, and wrote to her father.

"Let me a little expostulate with thee," he said. ". . . Thou art not come to the Berean-state that tried all things, and therefore not noble in the Christian sense. The Bereans were noble, for they judged not before examination." How well he remembered his father's saying: "Let us be like the noble Bereans!"

Before they left Duisburg a messenger, "a pretty, tender, young man," came from the Countess to tell them of her distress at the treatment they had received from her father. So they departed, pleased with message and messenger, but concerned for the Countess and the life she must lead with such a father.

On they went, now by wagon, now on foot; talking with inn-keepers and teachers and ministers, attorneys of the law and ladies of quality—one, to whom they were recommended by the Princess Elizabeth, though she was a woman of "great wit and high notions," talked so very much that it "was hard for us to obtain a true silence in which we could reach to her."

On the seventh of September, Penn was back in Amsterdam, where he found that during the month of their absence the meeting-house had been much enlarged. He stayed only three days before he went north again, this time with Jan Claus, a Dutch Friend, to Wiewart, where a very learned old lady, Anna Maria Schurman, lived with a little group of religious people somewhat like Quakers. From there he went on to Emden, where the little band of Friends whom he had left there six years ago was still stanch, in spite of unusually cruel persecution; and at length he came to Herwerden again, where he stayed for five days. But the Princess, though much drawn to Quakerism, never actually became a Friend.

From Herwerden to Wesel was two hundred miles, and they traveled three days and two nights without stopping, in a wagon which "was only covered with an old, ragged sheet." Ten people besides themselves were crowded into that wagon, and all night long as they lurched and bumped through the darkness, the other passengers alternately told vain stories and sang Lutheran hymns.

When they reached Wesel, Penn's long journey was almost over. Early in October he was in Amsterdam again, where he found dear George Fox and George Keith. They were all that was left of the original company, all the rest having gone home to England. On the twentieth they said farewell to the Dutch Friends who came to see them off, and went aboard the packet-boat at Brielle.

It was a miserable crossing; the weather was so stormy, with wind, rain, and sleet in driving gusts, that it took as long to cross from Brielle to Harwich as it had done to travel by wagon from Herwerden to Wesel. The pumps went day and night; some seamen were almost washed overboard, and the passengers got panicky.

Everybody was seasick. But at seven on the evening of the twenty-third, they landed safely at Harwich.

Penn and George Keith, anxious to push on to London and to Worminghurst, hired horses and rode ahead, leaving George Fox to follow by coach. Penn stopped in London for some meetings, and then, "I went to Worminghurst, my house in Sussex, where I found my dear wife, child, and family all well, blessed by the name of the Lord God of all the families of the earth." That evening they had a "sweet meeting" in which they were "truly glad together."

He had been gone three months, had traveled three thousand difficult miles, had preached innumerable sermons, had written four pamphlets, twelve weighty letters, and kept a journal!

20

"Spoil and Ruin"

FOR the next four years Penn's life was spent in two
separate compartments: Worminghurst, sunny with
love and peace; and the public arena of England, dark
with cruelty, conflict, and foreboding.

At Worminghurst life moved with a gentle and serious rhythm. On summer mornings the household got up
at five, in winter at seven. They had a meeting for
worship before breakfast at nine, and met again at eleven
for Bible reading; dinner was at twelve, and there was
an evening meeting before supper at seven. After supper
the servants reported on what they had done during the
day and were given orders for the next day. At ten
everybody went to bed.

This, at least, was Penn's plan for his household, but
whether it actually worked out that way is another
matter altogether. He himself was away much of the
time, and Gulielma was fine and gentle and charming,
she was industrious and kind, and Penn adored her—
but she was not systematic.

When Sunday came around, they went to meeting at
Coolham, four miles away, where part of a very old
farm house had been made into a meeting-house. William

Penn, when he was at home, walked or rode across the fields and through the orchard, but Gulielma went by carriage or, when the weather had been wet and mud was deep in the narrow road, by ox-cart. Sometimes, especially when they had guests, they held meeting in their own house; sometimes they went all the way to Horsham.

In March 1678, another baby came, a little girl whom they were so glad to have that they called her Letitia, which meant joy.

Much of the time this happy life at Worminghurst went on without Penn, who had to be in London. Things had come to a desperate pass in England, and because he was the man he was, brilliant, energetic, filled with a sense of responsibility, he could not stay quietly at home avoiding trouble; he must be out trying to make things better. Though some of his fellow Quakers criticized him for meddling in politics, he had a deep conviction that religious liberty and good government could not exist one without the other, and that when both were in danger, it was every man's duty to defend them who could.

England was torn between religion and religion, between the court and the people. Charles II believed that he was King by divine right, and he was determined to have his own way without interference from Parliament; he was secretly a Roman Catholic. Parliament, made up of Protestants, equally sure of its right to rule in England, had one means of control over the King: money. The King had to ask Parliament for money, and before they granted it to him they would make conditions to which he had to agree. To free himself from this control, Charles II of England entered upon a secret alliance with Louis XIV of France, also a Catholic, who in return gave him the money he needed.

Parliament and the country at large did not know of this secret treaty, but they suspected it. Distrusting France and terrified of Roman Catholicism, they passed drastic laws against all religious denominations outside of the Established Church. These laws, though aimed chiefly at the Catholics, hit the Protestant Non-Conformists too, and to relieve them a bill was proposed allowing them to escape the penalties if they would swear that they were not Catholics. The Quakers, of course, could not take oaths of any kind, and so they would get the benefit of all the punishments intended for Catholics.

In March 1678, William Penn went before two committees in the House of Commons and made speeches urging that Quakers be allowed to affirm, or give their word of honor, instead of swearing. It was unjust, he pointed out, they they should be punished for being something that they were not. Out of his fair-mindedness and his passionate belief in universal religious toleration, he had the courage to add, in a time when no one dared to appear friendly toward Catholics: "I would not be mistaken. I am far from thinking it fit that Papists should be whipped for their consciences because I exclaim against the injustice of whipping Quakers for Papists—for we must give the liberty we ask."

The Commons reported favorably on a bill to allow the Quakers to affirm, but before it could go through the House of Lords, the King prorogued Parliament, that is to say, he adjourned it until he should call it again. This he did because he was afraid that his alliance with the French was becoming known. In October, when Parliament met again, the secret treaty was brought to light and the King hastily dissolved Parliament altogether. Now a new one must be elected. It was a chance to start fresh, with sane and sensible men in office.

William Penn, who stood for religious toleration and justice in government, could not sit in Parliament because he could not take the oath, but he had a candidate who fulfilled all his ideals. Algernon Sidney, the great liberal whom he had met in exile in Italy in 1662, had been permitted to return to England on the death of his father in 1677, and was now living at the ancient seat of the Sidneys, Penshurst Place, in Kent, some thirty miles from Worminghurst. He now stood for Parliament for Guildford, and Penn threw himself heart and soul into campaigning for him.

The election lasted three weeks, and it was a sickening struggle against bribery and violence. Penn tirelessly made speeches and personal appeals, and when the day of voting finally came, Sidney won by a large majority. The court party, however, was strong enough to have Sidney ruled out on a technicality, and to give the seat in Parliament which he had won to the man whom he had defeated.

In spite of such tactics on the part of the Tories, or

King's party, the new Parliament was mainly made up of Whigs, or Liberals, and the King permitted it to sit only four months before he dissolved it.

In July there was another election and Sidney tried again. This time he stood for Bramber, in Sussex, near Worminghurst. Many were the conferences between him and William Penn; many the nights the two spent at Worminghurst or at Penshurst, planning their campaign. Again Sidney won the election—and again the court party had him thrown out and his opponent got the seat.

And all this time persecution was raging. The Quakers were caught between two fires. They suffered from the Protestant Whigs because they could not swear that they were not Catholics, and they suffered from the court party because they were Whig Non-Conformists. Thousands were in prison, where three hundred and fifty had died since King Charles came to the throne twenty years before. Those who were not in prison were fined twenty pounds a month, or two thirds of their estates, for not going to church; they were losing all they had. "The flocks have been taken out of the fold, the herd from the stall; not a cow left to give milk to the orphan, nor a bed for the widow to lie on; whole barns of corn swept away and not a penny returned." In Bristol Friars Meeting-House was wrecked; people were beaten and imprisoned, and even little children were put in the stocks.

For ten years Penn had given his life to the cause of

religious toleration, had preached it, written it, urged it before Parliament, judges, church, and people, had gone to prison for it. Now in these dark days it seemed more remote than ever. In despair he wrote: "There is no hope in England."

And then with unflagging determination and fresh vision, he turned to the new land across the seas.

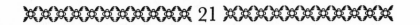

21

The Seed of a Nation

IN JUNE 1680, when cream-colored roses hung in masses over the deep red walls of Worminghurst and the warm breeze made flowing patterns in the hay-fields, William Penn sat down at his desk and wrote a petition to the King.

Charles II had owed his father money, for advances which the Admiral had made to him and for back-pay which the Admiral had never got. Now, with the interest that had accumulated, the sum amounted to sixteen thousand pounds. William Penn wrote and asked the King to give him, instead of the money, a tract of land in America, north of Maryland, south of New York, west of Delaware.

It was the land Josiah Coale had told him about, that dear George Fox had seen; it should be the land that he himself had dreamed of, a home for the persecuted, a government free to the people. "There may be room there," he thought, "though not here, for such an holy experiment." If the land was granted to him, he intended to call it New Wales, because he had heard it was a pretty, hilly, wooded country.

Months of uncertainty followed, of conferences, coun-

cils, committees; he must meet with the Duke of York's
agent and Lord Baltimore's agent about boundaries, with
the attorney general and the Lord Chief Justice of England; he must wait and hope; he must enlist the help of
his powerful friends. He had publicly supported Algernon
Sidney in his opposition to the court party in the last two
elections: would King Charles hold that against him? But
the Duke of York supported him, and the Earl of Sunderland, who was his old friend Robert Spencer with whom
he had traveled in France and Italy in the days of his
grand tour; and the King liked Admiral Penn's Quaker
son, whose honesty and sincerity were unquestioned. If
William Penn had asked for the sixteen thousand pounds
in money, he would never have got it, but since he was
willing, and even eager to take it out in wilderness
across the ocean, the King was disposed to settle his debt.
At length a charter was drafted, with a space left for the
King to fill in the name of the territory when he signed it.
It was a most impressive document, of parchment, written
in old English letters, underlined in red ink, with a border
of heraldic devices and the King's portrait at the top.

On March 4, 1681, the King signed it. And filled in
the name. The next day Penn wrote to his friend Robert
Turner of Dublin about it:

"5th, of 3rd mo., March 1681.
"Dear Friend:
"My true love in the Lord salutes thee and dear friends
that love the Lord's precious truth in those parts. Thine I

Charles II signs the Charter of Pennsylvania

have, and for my business here, know that after many wait-ings, watchings, solicitings, and disputes in council, this day my country was confirmed to me under the great seal of Eng-land, with large powers and privileges, by the name of Pennsylvania; a name the King would give it in honor of my father. . . . I proposed, when the Secretary, a Welshman, refused to have it called New Wales, Sylvania, and they added Penn to it; and though I much opposed it and went to the King to have it struck out and altered, he said it was past, and would not take it upon him; nor could twenty guineas move the under secretary to vary the name; for I feared lest it should be looked on as a vanity in me, and not as a respect in the King as it truly was, to my father, whom he often men-

tions with praise. Thou mayest communicate my grant to Friends and expect shortly my proposals.

"It is a clear and just thing, and my God that has given it me through many difficulties, will, I believe, bless and make it the seed of a nation. I shall have a tender care to the government, that it be well laid at first. No more now, but dear love in the truth.

"Thy true friend, Wm. Penn."

It was a disappointment about the name, but Penn was not the man to repine—not when he had just been made governor and sole proprietor of a piece of land nearly as large as all England, with power to make laws for it, subject to the King's approval, to appoint judges, and as "captain-general" to raise troops and make war, which last he had no intention of doing.

Now that the charter was signed, the business of Pennsylvania went forward with a surge of power and of strength. The King issued a declaration requiring all people now settled in the province to yield obedience to Penn; and to those people—some three thousand there were: Dutch and Swedes and English Quakers who had drifted over from New Jersey—Penn himself wrote a letter of reassurance and honest friendliness.

"My Friends:

"I wish you all happiness, here, and hereafter. These are to let you know that it hath pleased God, in his providence, to cast you within my lot and care. It is a business that, al-

*though I never undertook before, yet God hath given me an
understanding of my duty, and an honest mind to do it up-
rightly. I hope you will not be troubled at your change and the
King's choice, for you are now fixed at the mercy of no
governor that comes to make his fortune great; you shall be
governed by laws of your own making and live a free, and if
you will, a sober and industrious life. I shall not usurp the
right of any, or oppress his person. God has furnished me
with a better resolution and has given me his grace to keep
it. . . ."*

He sent his cousin William Markham, the son of his
father's sister, to America at once, to carry the King's
declaration and his own letter, and to act as his deputy
until he got there.

Before he could go to America himself, he had many
things to do in England. First of all he must get colonists.
He must let people know what kind of land it was, how
much it would cost, how they could get there, and what
sort of government they might expect there. So he
wrote "Some Account of the Province of Pennsylvania in
America," in which he described the country as best he
could; quoted the price of land (five thousand acres for
one hundred pounds, and an annual quit-rent of a shilling
for each hundred acres), the price of passage (six pounds
for each adult and fifty shillings for each child under
seven); and warned prospective colonists that they must
look for winter before summer and be willing to get

along without some of the conveniences that they had at home. As to the government, he was working out a plan. He wrote to Robert Turner:

"I propose that which is extraordinary, to leave myself and successors no power of doing mischief, that the will of one man may not hinder the good of an whole country."

During most of that summer of 1681 he was in London, occupied with the business of the colony, while at home at Worminghurst Guli was busy with a new baby, little Billy, born just ten days after the King signed the charter of Pennsylvania.

He had innumerable letters to write, an unending succession of people to see, deeds to sign, and every detail of his vast project to plan and to oversee. He thought of those days in his boyhood when his father had had a fleet of forty ships to equip for the expedition to Hispaniola— but this was a far greater undertaking than that.

He had Markham buy for him from the Indians six thousand acres of land on the Delaware near the falls, where he planned to make a real home for his family, and call it Pennsbury Manor. He made a deed granting twelve hundred and fifty acres to dear George Fox, for which he was to pay nothing but a rent of one peppercorn a year—"only if the same be lawfully demanded." He chose three commissioners to go out before him to assist Markham, and to carry out some of the ideas that were sizzling in his brain.

They sailed in October, and with them they carried a letter to the Indians.

"London, 18th of 10th mo. 1681.

"My Friends:

"There is one great God and power that hath made the world and all things therein, to whom you, and I, and all people owe their being and well-being, and to whom you and I must one day give an account for all that we have done in the world.

"The great God has written his law in our hearts, by which we are taught and commanded to love, and to help and to do good to one another. Now this great God hath been pleased to make me concerned in your part of the world; and the King of the country where I live hath given me a great province therein; but I desire to enjoy it with your love and consent, that we may always live together as neighbors and friends. . . . Now, I would have you well observe that I am very sensible of the unkindness and injustice which have been too much exercised toward you by the people of these parts of the world, who have sought themselves to make great advantages by you, rather than to be examples of justice and goodness unto you. . . . But I am not such a man, as is well known in my own country. I have great love and regard to you and desire to win and gain your love and friendship by a kind, just, and peaceable life; and the people I send are of the same mind, and shall in all things behave themselves accordingly. . . .

"I shall shortly come to see you myself, at which time we may more largely and freely confer and discourse of these matters. In the meantime I have sent my commissioners to treat with you about land and a firm league of peace. Let me

desire you to be kind to them and to the people and to receive the presents and tokens which I have sent you, as a testimony of my good will to you and of my resolution to live justly, peaceably, and friendly with you.

"I am, your loving friend,

"William Penn."

He realized that on his success in establishing friendly relations with the Indians depended the success of his holy experiment; that a government which is good because it is based upon religion must begin by dealing fairly and lovingly with the original owners of the land. Besides sending this letter to the Indians, he gave his commissioners specific instructions about dealing with them.

"Be tender of offending the Indians. . . . To soften them to me, and the people, let them know that you are come to sit down lovingly with them." With the understanding and true courtesy that made Quaker Penn, in spite of his thee and thou and his stubborn hat, warmly received by the great and ceremonious of the kingdom, he added: "Be grave; they love not to be smiled on."

His friendliness and his concern for the Indians were genuine; it was not a matter of policy—though it proved in the end to be the best of all astute policies. He was willing to make sacrifices for it. A trading-company offered him six thousand pounds for a monopoly of trade with the Indians, but knowing that if he accepted he would lose his power to defend the Indians from exploitation and unfair dealings, he refused flatly, saying he would not "so defile what came to me clean."

With the commissioners on one of the two ships that went out to Pennsylvania that autumn, went also Penn's directions for the laying out of a "great town" beside the Delaware, a town that was to cover ten thousand acres, with straight wide streets, and large lots so that each house might be surrounded by "gardens or orchards or fields, that it may be a green country town, which will never be burnt and always wholesome." Only too well he remembered the plague and the fire, and what they had done to London.

In the midst of all this activity, he never forgot that he was a Quaker as well as the governor of a great province, and he made a trip to Bristol on a religious mission, wrote a tract designed to smooth out some differences between two groups of the Society of Friends, and made great efforts to put a stop to the persecution that was raging.

Soon after his return from a trip to the west of England, he had a narrow escape from an imprisonment that might have played havoc with his American plans. Once again the meeting at Gracechurch Street was attended by William Penn, and a band of soldiers. Once again William Penn, paying no more attention to the soldiers than if they had been a swarm of flies, rose to speak. The constable, waving his staff, ordered him to cease speaking and be arrested. Penn calmly finished what he had to say. George Fox, who was there too, rose to preach after him, received the same command from the officers, and went right on talking with the same calm. The constable, when he had heard them both out, was so genuinely impressed by what they had said and by the seriousness and serenity of the whole meeting that he went away without arresting either William Penn or George Fox.

During the spring months of 1682, Penn wrote his Frame of Government for Pennsylvania. He went back to Worminghurst, there in the beauty and peace of its atmosphere to marshal his thoughts and accomplish what was to be perhaps the greatest task of his life. There too came people to help him with discussion and advice, some who were real statesmen in the world, and some obscure members of his own society who yet had the broad and far-reaching minds and tolerant spirits that such an undertaking required. Algernon Sidney gave him counsel, both at Penshurst and at Worminghurst; and John Locke, who had been a don at Christ Church when he was an undergraduate, and who had twelve years ago drawn up a constitution for Lord Shaftesbury's colony of South Carolina, made marginal notes on Penn's Frame.

When it was finished, Algernon Sidney complained that Penn had kept too much power to himself, and John Locke objected that he had given entirely too much power to the people. It is interesting to remember that although John Locke's rigid, aristocratic constitution for Carolina broke down under the first strain, Penn's flexible, democratic Frame of Government for Pennsylvania survived to be the model for most of the state constitutions and for the constitution of the United States as well.

In the preface to it, he stated once again, clearly and strongly, his fundamental beliefs about government: "Government seems to me a part of religion itself, a thing sacred in its institution and end. . . . And government is free to the people under it, whatever be the frame, where the laws rule and the people are a party to those laws; and more than this is tyranny, oligarchy, or confusion. . . . As governments are made and moved by men, so by them they are ruined too. Wherefore governments rather depend upon men than men upon governments. Let men be good, and the government cannot be bad. If it be ill, they will cure it. But if men be bad, let the government be ever so good, they will endeavor to warp and spoil it to their turn."

From its very beginning, Pennsylvania had religious liberty, a council and assembly elected by the people to make the laws, trial by jury, and a penal system designed to reform, not merely to punish, the evil doer. Whereas in England at that time there were more than two hundred capital offenses, in Pennsylvania a man could be condemned to death for only two crimes: murder and treason.

The summer of 1682, for all its tense expectancy of high and hopeful adventure, brought sorrow. Lady Penn died at Worminghurst in June, and Penn's grief for his mother was so intense that for a short time he was actually ill. Not long after that Mary Penington, now a

widow, came there to visit, looking so white and frail
that everyone realized without needing to be told, that
she too had only a little while to live. If Gulielma's going
to America with Penn had ever been seriously thought
of, it was now out of the question. She would have to
follow him later. . . .

The time of going was near at hand. Penn had done all
that he could do in England, and his Pennsylvania needed
him. The ship *Welcome* was to sail on August 30.

And now Penn, who had planned so wisely and far-
sightedly for his colony, took loving thought for the
family that he was leaving behind. Pennsylvania was
three thousand miles across the ocean; on the seas were
storms and pirates, on land those unknown savages;
everywhere was the still more deadly and insidious
enemy, disease. Unafraid for himself, he thought of his
little flock, and tried to foresee what of guidance and
counsel from him would be a help to them if he should
not see them again in this world. Simply and lovingly he
wrote them a letter.

"My dear wife!

*"Remember thou wast the love of my youth, and much the
joy of my life; the most beloved as well as the most worthy of
all my earthly comforts: and the reason of that love was more
thy inward than thy outward excellencies, which yet were
many. . . .*

"Be diligent in meetings for worship and business; stir

up thyself and others therein; it is thy duty and place: and let meetings be kept once a day in the family to wait upon the Lord, who has given us much time for ourselves . . . and, my dearest, to make thy family matters easy to thee, divide thy time and be regular: it is easy and sweet. . . . Cast up thy income and see what it daily amounts to: by which thou mayest be sure to have it in thy sight and power to keep within compass. . . .

"And now, my dearest, let me recommend to thy care my dear children; abundantly beloved of me as the Lord's blessings, and the sweet pledges of our mutual and endeared affection."

And to his children, words of wise and tender advice which they were too young now to understand:

"Love not money nor the world; use them only and they will serve you; but if you love them, you serve them. . . . Be gentle and humble in your conversation. . . . In making friends consider well first; and when you are fixed be true. . . . Watch against anger, neither speak nor act in it; for like drunkenness it makes a man a beast and throws people into desperate inconveniences. . . . Finally, my children, love one another. . . .

"So farewell to my thrice dearly beloved wife and children! Yours, as God pleaseth, in that which no waters can quench, no time forget, no distance wear away, but remains forever,

"William Penn."

So he stood on the threshold of his great adventure. He was thirty-eight years old, tall, athletic in build, good looking, a strong and magnetic personality.

Confidently he strode forward, and, trusting him, people followed.

22

Onas

A LITTLE ship, the *Welcome;* it weighed only three hundred tons. It carried a hundred colonists and all their goods; all the necessary things—the spades and axes and plowshares that they took to break ground and build houses; and the precious things—the cupboards and beds and Bibles and silver candlesticks without which they could not make a home; it carried all the provisions they would need for two months on the Atlantic—live cows and chickens and geese, dried herbs and codfish, chocolate, spices, ship's biscuits. One man took a mill with him, knocked down in parts; and William Penn, besides his chests and furniture, was taking paneling and woodwork for his house at Pennsbury, and fine horses for his stable. The little ship, so heavily laden, rode low in the water, and steady; and day after day favoring winds blew it westward across the ocean.

Justly laid and seasonably timed this project had been, and yet, in spite of all the care and forethought, tragedy, unsuspected, came aboard at Deal. When they had been only a few days at sea, one of the passengers came down with small pox and soon, like wildfire, the dread disease went raging through the ship. In those cramped and crowded quarters, one after another was laid low in sickness and misery. Penn, who had had small pox when he was three years old, turned to and worked tirelessly in caring for the sick and comforting the sorrowful. He gave liberally from his own stores of medicines and other necessities, and still more generously of his strength and kindness. Again and again his heart was torn for his anguished people, many of whom had been his neighbors in Sussex. Thirty-one out of the hundred died and were buried at sea, between the land that they had left and the land toward which they had turned with such high hopes.

Hardly one of those who were left was not weakened by illness or sorrow.

When, late in October, twelve leagues still from the shore, they "smelled land," and thought it sweet as a new-blown flower garden, relief and thankfulness welled up in their heavy hearts, and hope was set alight once more in tear-dimmed eyes. The voyage was over, and this land that they had reached was beautiful.

Up the wide pathway of the Delaware they sailed. On either side, the low-lying woods were ablaze with yellow and scarlet and russet; flocks of wild ducks wheeled and soared in the unutterably blue sky overhead; the clear, crisp, sun-drenched breeze was like wine. It made Penn think of the air in the south of France, at Saumur.

On October 27 they landed at New Castle, the little Dutch town that George Fox had visited. William

Markham, full of news of the province and eager for news from England, was there to meet them, and there they spent the night. The next morning Governor Penn met the magistrates in the little courthouse, showed his deeds from the Duke of York, and took seizin of New Castle and the surrounding country in the age-old ceremony of turf and twig and water and soil of the river Delaware. The three counties east of Maryland, on the Delaware, which are now the state of Delaware, were the Duke of York's Territories which Penn had bought and which were subject to his rule, but not part of Pennsylvania. He received pledges of faith from their inhabitants, gave his promise to deal fairly with them, and recommissioned all their magistrates. So he made his first friendships in his new country.

That afternoon he went aboard the *Welcome* once more, and sailed twenty miles farther up the river to Upland, the first town in his own Pennsylvania.

Thirty-four years before, the Swedes had settled Upland, and named it for a province on the Gulf of Bothnia. Here in 1681 the *John and Sarah* and the *Bristol Factor* had landed, and, the river freezing over almost immediately afterwards, here Friends had stayed all winter. Some were still there, eager to welcome the Governor and the new arrivals. The little town was full of bustle and excitement. Here he spent the night, and here next morning, which was Sunday, he went to his first meeting for worship in Pennsylvania. A "precious meeting" it must have been, in the little frontier house, with the wide river flowing past on one side and the vast forest stretching away to unknown distances on the other.

The name of Upland he changed to Chester, to mark the coming of a change in government, and to all its Dutch and Swedish townsfolk he gave citizenship forthwith. But Chester was not to be his "great citie." Once more he took the river, this time in what was to be his favorite way of traveling in Pennsylvania, in an open barge with a sail and a crew of eight, a boatswain, a coxswain, and six rowers. William Markham went with him, and some Friends from the *Welcome*.

November had come, and the yellow leaves had drifted to the ground; the scarlet ones had dulled to russet, and bare branches were violet in the distance. Crows cawed. The Governor's barge, drawing toward the western shore of the river, sailed past the mouth of the Schuylkill and came to Coaquannock, the high ground lying between the two rivers where he had commanded his commissioners to lay out his city. Philadelphia, city of brotherly love, he had decided to call it.

As they drew closer to the site that he had chosen but never seen, Penn's heart beat faster. Quite suddenly the wind-ruffled river around him was dotted with boats; one after another they slipped out from the woods along the shore, swift canoes filled with dark, silent, redskinned men. Black glistening locks with a couple of bright quills stuck through a top-knot; strong, lean, inscrutable faces; blankets over broad shoulders, bare, reddish brown, hard-muscled arms and legs: these were

"Penn . . . sprang up and outran and outjumped them all"

the Indians in whose forests they had come to live, whose
streams they would fish. They came in silent canoes with
strong swift strokes of the paddle, and looked, and
slipped away again. Later there would be a ceremony of
welcome, but not now.

The barge put in at the place where Dock Creek,
cutting through the high banks, made a natural harbor.
On one side pine trees grew tall against the sky, their
needles glistening in the sunshine and moving in the
wind; on the other a house was already going up, a long
plain substantial house of heavy beams, filled in with
brick. George Guest was building it, and when it was
done he was going to call it the Blue Anchor Tavern.

Here the Friends who had come out before him had gathered to welcome William Penn.

Now, and for the month to come, he was busy every moment of the day. The Indians who lived hereabouts wished to make a ceremony to welcome him. Cordially he went among them, walked with the chiefs, sat on the ground with the young men; ate with them their roasted acorns and hominy. In high feather they began to show off before him, running and jumping; whereupon William Penn, who had won at foot-races and hurdles in his Chigwell school days, sprang up and outran and outjumped them all. And doing so, won their hearts. A white woman who was watching remembered that day when she was more than a hundred years old, and wrote that William Penn was "the handsomest, best looking, liveliest gentleman" she had ever seen.

He made his headquarters in Shackamaxon, a mile or so from the tract that was to be Philadelphia, in the house of Thomas Fairman, who obligingly moved his family to Tacony, a settlement to the north; and from there he wrote letters, attended meetings, and watched over the pride and darling of his heart, his new city.

Already the chief streets had been laid out, but he made some changes. The wide street running north and south he moved westward so that it might be on the highest ground, and he called it Broad Street. Where it intersected the wide street running east and west, the name of which he changed from Union to High, he laid out ten acres for public buildings and a park. In the middle of each of the four quarters of the city he saved out eight acres for a square with public walks, like Moor Fields in London. The streets running north and south he said should be numbered, and those running east and west should be named for the trees of the forest —Walnut, Chestnut, Pine, Sassafras.

He rode with Thomas Fairman to Indian villages to see the chiefs and to ask them to call their people to a great conference, as he had promised in his letter he would do. Going still farther afield, he went in his barge to the Falls of Delaware, and from there rode across New Jersey to New York, where he paid a call of state upon the governor and visited the Friends' meetings in Long Island. All along the way, wherever he passed a settlement, he stopped and made friends with the people there, for he was a proprietor of both East and West New Jersey now. When Sir George Carteret had died, early in the year, Penn and eleven others had bought East New Jersey from his estate. Robert Barclay of Ury was governor of East Jersey, though he never saw it and a deputy ruled in his place.

On the way home Penn saw his broad acres on the Delaware, and planned how he would set his house on the high ground where an arm of the river almost encircled it.

Late in November, when the Indian runners had had time to go out with messages, three tribes gathered for the treaty conference: the Lenni Lenape, the Mingoes, who were a branch of the Iroquois, and the Shawnees, from the region of the Susquehanna. Shackamaxon was the meeting-ground—Shackamaxon, which meant place of the sachems, or chiefs, where for years the Indian kings had held their council.

Here, under a tall elm, the tribes gathered to meet the great chief whom they had already learned to call Onas, the Indian word for quill or pen. They came in full ceremonial array of buckskins and feathered headdress; solemnly and in silence they formed a semi-circle before the council fire, the chiefs in front with their councilors, the old men on either side, and the young men behind. In the center was Taminent the Great Sachem, wearing a horn in his headdress as the sign of his power. They came without weapons.

Then Penn approached, with his councilors, Markham and Holmes and others; Penn, tall and handsome and grave, wearing a sky-blue silk scarf to show his rank. Gifts were brought and spread upon the ground.

Taminent greeted the Englishmen. Through an interpreter he invited them to speak; the nations would listen.

William Penn stepped forward.

"The Great Spirit," he said, "who made me and you, who rules the heavens and the earth, and who knows the innermost thoughts of men, knows that I and my friends have a hearty desire to live in peace and friendship with you, and to serve you to the utmost of our power. It is not our custom to use hostile weapons against our fellow creatures, for which reason we have come unarmed. Our

object is not to do injury, and thus provoke the Great
Spirit, but to do good.

"We are met on the broad pathway of good faith and
good will, so that no advantage is to be taken on either
side, but all to be openness, brotherhood, and love."

Then he set forth the points of the treaty, and explained each one; how all paths should be open and free
to both white men and Indians; how neither should believe false reports of each other, but should come first
like brethren and inquire of each other; how the doors of
white men's houses should be open to Indians, and the
houses of the Indians open to white men; and finally how
both white men and Indians should tell their children
and their children's children of this friendship between
them, so that it might ever endure and grow stronger.

"I will not do as the Marylanders did," he finished,
"that is, call you children or brothers only; for parents
are apt to whip their children too severely, and brothers
sometimes will differ; neither will I compare the friendship between us to a chain, for the rain may rust it or a
tree may fall and break it, but I will consider you as the
same flesh and blood with the Christians, and the same as
if one man's body were to be divided into two parts."

He stopped. The smoke of the council fire curled up
into the clear, clean air; the shadows on the frost-hard
ground were light and sharp; a squirrel chattered in the
elm over their heads. The Indians spoke among themselves.

Then a chief stepped forward, and taking Penn by the

hand, pledged the good faith and friendship of the Indians so long as "the creeks and rivers run, and while the sun, moon, and stars endure."

The treaty was recorded in a wampum belt, in which the Indians wove a picture of a man in a hat clasping hands with a man without a hat—this treaty which the great French philosopher Voltaire said was the only treaty never sworn to and never broken. Kept it was, so long as Penn's influence and the influence of the Quakers lasted in the colony.

The doors of the white man's house were open to the Indians, who came for breakfast, and brought gifts of wild turkey and venison. In some of the remote plantations, Friends going to Yearly Meeting in Philadelphia left their children behind in the care of the Indians, and felt safe about them.

And long after Onas, their "great friend," had gone to the happy hunting ground, the Lenni Lenape and the Iroquois and the Shawnees remembered and honored his name. For their fathers had loved him.

23

Four Seasons in Pennsylvania

WINTER

"From December to the beginning of the month called March we had sharp, strong, frosty weather; not foul, thick, black weather as our northeast winds bring with them in England, but a sky as clear as in the summer, and the air dry, cold, piercing, and hungry."

THE first Assembly met in Chester on December 4. It elected a speaker, made a ruling against "superfluous and tedious speeches" which might well be copied by congresses today, voted to reduce the number of its members, granted the petition of the three lower counties to be united with Pennsylvania, drew up the Great Law, a code of seventy laws which included Penn's original forty—and adjourned after four days. Most admirable dispatch!

Four days later the Governor of Pennsylvania with his advisers set out for Maryland to meet Lord Baltimore and discuss boundaries, a thorny question that was to trouble the two provinces for ninety years to come.

They met at West River on the Chesapeake, and it

205

was an occasion full of ceremony and civilities. Lord Baltimore, aristocratic, autocratic, and irritable, was there with all the most important men of his colony in attendance, and the little town in the wilderness was bright with velvets and laces, and plumed hats, with sleek horses and shiny harness, with servants in livery. English voices rang through the wintry air in elaborate phrases of courtesy. The wooden mansions built among the forest trees were all prepared for visitors; oak and apple logs crackled on wide hearths; the best silver was set forth; the furniture from England well polished. In the kitchens the good things that this rich new land provided sizzled on the spit or bubbled in great iron pots, or stood waiting in rows on scrubbed pine tables and in decanters on the sideboard: turkey and pheasant and venison, cranberries, pickled oysters, pies of pumpkin and of plum, wine brought in hogsheads from Madeira and wine made from the "savage green grape" of the American woods.

To the conference came William Penn in his sober Quaker clothes—made of the very best materials and by the best of London tailors—tall and handsome, courtly in his bearing. "I know of no religion," he said once, "that destroys courtesy, civility, and kindness." With him were Markham, who being no Quaker, could peacock it with the grandest of the Marylanders, and two or three Friends in sober browns and grays.

On the second day, when all the greetings and feastings were over, the two governors and their councils gathered around a big table to discuss boundary lines.

The trouble was that the Commissioners of Trade and Plantations in London, who had assigned these territories, knew very little about geography in America. They had given Lord Baltimore two degrees beginning at Watkins Point and stretching north; they had given Penn three degrees beginning at the New York line and stretching south—and there simply were not five degrees altogether between New York and Watkins Point. If Lord Baltimore had got all he claimed, Philadelphia would have been in Maryland, and if Penn had got all he claimed, Baltimore would have been in Pennsylvania!

Furthermore, Lord Baltimore claimed that the three lower counties (now the state of Delaware) belonged to him, whereas Penn had bought them from the Duke of York, who had two separate charters for them from the King.

They talked the matter over, came to no agreement, and having decided, amicably enough, to postpone discussion till the spring, they parted. The next ten days Penn spent in visiting Friends' meetings in Maryland, and by the end of the month was back in Chester, from where he wrote with a sigh of satisfaction: "Oh, how sweet is the quiet of these parts, freed from the anxious and troublesome solicitations, hurries, and perplexities of woeful Europe!"

Philadelphia was growing like the lusty babe she was. Twenty-three ships had come since summer, and houses were springing up on all the straight new streets. Some of the colonists brought the frames of their houses with them; some, the poorer ones, lived in caves dug out in the high river banks until they could chop down trees and build homes for themselves. Every carpenter had more work than he could do, and there was constant lamentation that there were not more carpenters in the colony. A baby was born to a family named Key, and Penn, to celebrate the arrival of this first real Philadelphian, deeded to him a lot all his own in the center of the city. His name was John, but all through his long life he was known as First-Born Key.

Night and day the Governor was busy, spending his time, his money, his strength untiringly on this great, this amazing undertaking of his: one man to lay out a city in rich, new, unspoiled land, one man to build a ship of state according to his own plans and launch it himself on the wide waters of the future! No one knew better than William Penn, however, that one man could not do it all alone. Men do not depend upon governments as governments depend upon men. The success of his Pennsylvania rested after all on the people who were to live there, and on their descendants. To an old friend who, with the early Quakers' uncompromising concern to speak the truth as he saw it, had accused him of "sitting down in greatness," William Penn wrote: "It is now in Friends' hands. Through my travail, faith, and patience it came. If Friends here keep to God in the justice, mercy, equity, and fear of the Lord, their enemies will be their footstool; if not, their heirs and my heirs too will lose all and desolation will follow." His holy experi-

ment succeeded partly because it was justly laid and seasonably timed by him, and partly because his first colonists
were fine and true. When fear and greed and dishonesty
grew among the people, then Pennsylvania suffered.

Penn loved it—all the rush, the activity, the planning,
and the place itself. He wrote to Lord Culpeper, who
had just come from England to be governor of Virginia:
"I like it so well that a plentiful estate and a great acquaintance on the other side have no charms to remove;
my family being once fixed with me, and if no other thing
occur I am like to be an adopted American." (If Guli
were only there with him!)

Pennsbury Manor was being built on a generous
scale: sixty feet long and thirty wide, three stories high,
with a porch in front with rails and banisters, and a wide
walk from the front door to the river, with gardens on
either side.

He sent beaver and otter skins to England to make
hats and muffs for the King, the Duke of York, and
Lord Hyde. "'Tis the heart and not the gift that gives
acceptance."

SPRING

*"From that month (March) to the month called June, we
enjoyed a sweet spring, no gusts but gentle showers and a
fine sky."*

The Assembly and Council met early in March in
Philadelphia. They made Penn's first Frame of Govern-

ment into a constitution, which they called the New
Charter, though there was nothing new in it but the
reduction of the number of members which they had
decided on in December, and the change of the triple
vote allowed to the Governor in Council meetings to a
single one. They offered to put a tax on all exports and
imports for the benefit of the Governor, but Penn, with
his large generosity, declined it. His expenses had been
heavy and were to be still heavier, but he would not have
his young province taxed for him.

Pennsbury was ready for him in April, still so new
that it smelled of fresh-cut boards, with oceans of mud
outside where some day there would be courtyards and
gardens; but the river flowed by, a silver pathway for his
beloved barge, and the woods were full of flowers as
lovely as any he had seen in London gardens.

In May he met Lord Baltimore again, as they had
planned, to talk about that boundary line, but again, in
all civility, they could not agree. Lord Baltimore said
he was not well and the weather was sultry, and he was
not ready to make a treaty yet.

So Penn came home and treated with the Indians instead, for some land that he wanted near Neshaminy
Creek. According to the terms of the purchase, his land
was to extend "as far back as a man could walk in three
days." They walked it out together, Penn and some
Friends and some Indian chiefs, walking not too fast and
stopping now and then to smoke their pipes (the Indians,
not Penn, who, like the master of the Chigwell School,

was no puffer of tobacco), to eat biscuits and cheese, and to drink a bottle of wine. For a day and a half in the warm bright June weather they walked through the woods on the edge of the Delaware, until, reaching a big spruce at the mouth of Baker's Creek thirty miles from where they started, Penn decided that this was as much land as he needed for the present, and the rest could be walked out later. (And so it was, but not until fifty years later, when Penn was no longer there to insist that his Indian friends got fair treatment. The Governor of that day, who was, sad to say, his own son Thomas, hired three runners who covered eighty-six miles in a day and a half; and for the first time these Indians felt cheated by the white men, and resentful.)

A much longer trip than this Penn made among the Indians when he rode a hundred miles into the Susquehanna valley. Only twenty or thirty years before, the Indians of this same region had descended upon the Marylanders, burning and killing and torturing; but Penn went among them unarmed and without fear.

With his skill in languages he had picked up enough of their tongue to mingle with them without an interpreter, and when he went deep into the Indian country, he went as a friend and as an honored guest. At night he slept in Indian wigwams, built of barks of trees set on poles; he ate with them sitting on his heels on the ground. After the evening meal of corn cakes roasted in the ashes, and peas and beans, and trout fresh from the rivers, they would sit together around the fire, while the deep woods rustled in the darkness behind them. The young men danced in the firelight, the older men passed from hand to hand the gifts that Penn had brought, and the women crept close to see.

"Let them have justice and you win them," he wrote later. But he himself gave them more than justice; he gave them trust and friendship; and he won from them love.

All through the spring the new country poured out its gifts to the people who had come to live there: shad running in the cold swift rivers in March and April; wild pigeons in flocks so great that the air was dark with them; strawberries spicy and fragrant on sunny hillsides. The rich black soil made the seeds from England spring up in fat green rows in the new garden plots.

SUMMER

"[From June to August] we have had extraordinary heats, yet mitigated sometimes by cool breezes."

Never was England at its hottest anything like this! But the Indian corn grew tall and its silky tassels turned from green to palest amber and then frizzled and browned in the blazing sun. Peaches and plums and apples hung heavy on the trees. Muskmelons and watermelons swelled on their sprawling vines, and in the deep woods, which were now still and hot and dry and smelled of thick leaves and weeds, grapes slowly ripened in vast tangles and festoons from tree to tree.

The Indians held harvest festivals to honor the God in whom they believed "without the help of metaphysics," and to one of these Penn went. Beside a great spring they gathered, where the shade of trees and the cold water over moss and stones made a damp freshness in the August day. There they feasted on venison and hot cakes of new corn wrapped in leaves and baked in ashes, and after feasting they danced.

Two braves in the middle of a ring began the cantico, singing and drumming on a board; the others danced around in a circle, doing different steps but all keeping time to the deep, wild rhythm of the low-voiced singing and the steady drumming. Now and then an exultant shout went up in the hot August stillness of the woods.

Those who came to watch brought small presents with them, of wampum, which was made of polished fish bones, black and white. The black was most precious.

On the twentieth of August the ship *America* arrived from London, bringing two men who were to mean much to Penn, and to Pennsylvania. One was Thomas Lloyd, a Welsh physician who had studied at Oxford, a strong and able man and a Quaker. The other was a young German, pale and quiet, with a big nose and far-seeing eyes—Francis Daniel Pastorius. He came from Frankfurt as the agent of the German Company to buy fifteen thousand acres in Pennsylvania, and during the eight weeks on the *America* he had been convinced of Quakerism.

Penn hailed his coming with joy. In a way he had been

lonely here, for there had been no one who could talk with him about the things he knew and loved to talk about. "Our heads are dull," he had written to Lord Hyde. "What fineness transportation will give, I know not, but our hearts are good and our hands strong." But this new arrival had studied at four German universities; had made the grand tour as tutor to a "noble young spark" through France, Switzerland, Italy, Holland, and England; had read Penn's books, and compared Barclay's *Apology* to "pure pearls, to rubies and diamonds." They were friends at once.

"He often sends me an invitation to dine with him," wrote Pastorius, "also to walk or ride in his always edifying company." So much did Pastorius like and revere his new friend that his pen, although it was made of an eagle's feather which an Indian had given him, was "much too weak to express the lofty virtues of this Christian."

When Penn was not at Pennsbury Manor, he lived in a frame house on his lot on Chestnut Street between Front and Second, and there he entertained many visitors; now a Friend from England; now six Indian chiefs at once; and regularly, twice in every week, Francis Daniel Pastorius, who, with the servants he had brought from Germany, lived for his first two years in Philadelphia quite comfortably in a cave in the river bank.

In the midst of all these new joys and interests there were thoughts that troubled. Word came that Lord Baltimore had sent his story of the boundary dispute to England, and that it was none too accurate. Accordingly

Penn sent Markham to London with letters to everybody he knew, to the King and the Duke, to Henry
Sidney, Algernon's younger brother who was much at
court, to Lord Sunderland, and to Lord Hyde. As he
himself said with the ironic humor that occasionally
emerged from his Quakerliness: "Though I hope God
will prosper our honest care and industry, yet a friend
at court is a good thing."

News came too that some people in England were
going about saying that William Penn was dead—and
"dead a Jesuit too." Perhaps no order in the Roman
Catholic Church was so much suspected and feared in
the England of the seventeenth century as the Jesuits.
Penn, when he wrote his long letter describing Pennsylvania to the Free Society of Traders, began by referring
to this rumor. "To the great sorrow and shame of the
inventors," he wrote, "I am still alive and no Jesuit; and,
I thank God, very well."

It was a charge that was to bob up again and trouble
him. Now he laughed at it and shook his head, and, turning to the great absorbing business of his colony, dismissed it from his mind.

AUTUMN

*"Of the fall, I found it . . . as we have it usually in England
in September, or, rather, like an English mild spring."*

On October 8 thirty-four German Quakers arrived on
the *Concord* from Crefeld on the Rhine. On the twelfth

Penn issued to them and to Pastorius a warrant for six thousand acres of land. On the twenty-fifth of the month, the thirteen men of the company (of the other twenty-one, ten were women, ten children, and one a "youth") met in Pastorius's dug-out and drew lots for the sites of their future homes. Though Pastorius stayed for the present in Philadelphia, the Crefelders would not wait; they made their way up the Schuylkill River to the Wissahickon Creek, then up the Wissahickon till they came to the land that was set apart for them. Here along a winding Indian trail, they built their houses of rough stone and laid out their fields in which they would raise flax for linen, and grapes for wine. They called their settlement Germantown.

In December Penn, deciding that the children must not grow up ignorant, engaged a man named Enoch Flower, twenty years a schoolmaster in England, to teach his little Philadelphians to read and write and cast accounts. Flower's charges were not exorbitant: "To learn to read English, four shillings by the quarter; to learn to read and write, six shillings; to learn to read, write and cast accounts, 8sh.; to board a scholar, diet, washing, lodging and schooling, ten pounds for one whole year."

And so Penn's second winter was beginning. From England Stephen Crisp wrote to him with tender concern: "I have had a sense of the various spirits and intricate cares and multiplicity of affairs and these of various kinds which daily attend thee, enough to drink up thy spirit and tire thy soul. . . ."

But it was not the multiplicity of Penn's affairs in Philadelphia that was to drink up his spirit and tire his soul. Clouds were gathering in England.

24

The Governor Sails

LETTERS from England brought disturbing news. Guli
had been ill, so ill that Thomas Ellwood had been
sent for. He was slated to appear before a magistrate to
answer for a tract which he had written, but when he
explained that Madame Penn was ill and needed him,
the judge let him off altogether—so much did everyone
love and respect Gulielma Penn. The illness passed, and
Guli wrote that she was better, but Penn was worried.
Was she really as well as she said, or was she trying to
spare him anxiety? All through this year and a half he
had kept hoping that she would soon come out to him,
but now he knew that she could not do it unless he went
back to fetch her. He began to feel restless, and his
thoughts turned constantly toward England.

There was something else. His old friend Algernon
Sidney had been executed on the charge of having taken
part in the Rye House plot against the King. No one
seemed to know whether he had actually done what he
was accused of, but on December 7 he had walked
steadily to the scaffold, declared that he had made his
peace with God, that he came not to talk but to die, and
so gave up his life on the side of the people against the

Worminghurst—Penn's home in Sussex

King. Even those who were on the other side recognized his courage and his sincerity. Penn, who had gone through two campaigns with him and spent hours discussing and arguing over his plan for Pennsylvania, heard with a heavy heart this news of Sidney's death. Things were not right in England when such men went to execution. Soon, in letters from this person and from that, came word of fresh and more severe persecution of Non-Conformists.

In Pennsylvania the boundary dispute took a sudden and alarming turn. Colonel George Talbot of Maryland with a company of armed men marched into the Territories, took by force some land near New Castle, built a log fort, established a garrison in it, and called on the settlers in the surrounding country to acknowledge Lord

Baltimore as their governor and pay rent to him! When
the President of New Castle with the chief magistrates
went to the fort to ask what such a war-like invasion
meant, Talbot covered them with his guns and replied
that he had Lord Baltimore's commission for what he did.

The people from New Castle, "being old experi-
enced" men, managed to keep calm enough not to rush
home to get their own muskets; instead they pointed out
that such proceedings were entirely illegal, and took
steps to get the matter settled by law.

Then Penn, trying to deal directly with Lord Baltimore, found that he had already departed for England to
tell his story to the King first. Now Penn knew what he
would have to do. He must go to England, and at once.

There were a thousand things to do first. With his
usual energy he rushed at them. He made Thomas
Lloyd president of the Council in his place, and Markham, who was still in England, was to be its secretary
when he returned. James Harrison he made steward of
Pennsbury Manor, to care for it and develop it while he
was gone.

He did not expect to be gone long. He would soon
have this boundary business settled; then a little while to
do what he could for those who were being persecuted, a
little while to prepare his family and wind things up at
Worminghurst, and then he and Guli and the children
would come to Pennsbury Manor to stay.

On August 12, 1684, less than two years since he had

left England, he boarded the *Endeavor* and sailed down the Delaware. His mind, as he drew farther and farther away from the scattered roofs among the trees, was on his Philadelphia, that growing green country town of his own making. Nearly three hundred houses it had now, the meeting-house was built, young businesses were springing up on all sides. Next year there would be a printing press. Two years ago there had been only the streets marked out, and Guest's new house going up on Dock Creek.

"And thou, Philadelphia," he wrote in his farewell to it, "the virgin settlement of this province, named before thou wert born, what love, what care, what service, and what travail had been to bring thee forth and preserve thee from such as would abuse and defile thee."

His people whom he left behind mourned his going. "I wish with all my heart," wrote one, "that all the governors upon the earth were such as he is." But they too expected that he would be back soon. They had no idea how long it was to be, or how sorely they would need him, before he came again.

The crossing this time took forty-seven days, and there was no illness on board. On October 6 William Penn landed at Wonder in Sussex, just seven miles from his home.

He found his family well. For a little while, all Pennsylvania faded into a dream beside that great, that joyful fact. Guli was older, and a little worn looking, but she was his same Guli, tender and shining eyed. His three children, four and six and eight, like stair-steps, were healthy, and grown almost beyond recognizing.

Happiness shimmered over Worminghurst that evening as he had seen heat shimmer over a green field of Indian corn.

But two years had passed over them all, and time changes all things, except love. More than the three thousand miles of the Atlantic Ocean had separated William Penn from his little brood. He had conceived and guided a city and a state as other men of his age bring up a family; Philadelphia and Pennsylvania for two years had taken all his mind and strength, they had been more than children to him. Now Springett, who was eight, was the only one of his own whom he really knew, and him he knew partly because the little boy was so much like Guli, slender and fine and sensitive. Tishe was a plump, pretty little girl, fond of her doll and intent on her frocks and ribbons, guardedly polite to this great stranger who was her father. Billy at four had learned how to get his own way by terrifying outbursts of temper.

He watched them as they hung around him, shyly studying his face and returning smile for smile, plucking at his sleeve and asking in their flute-like little voices for more stories about the Indians. He wrote to Margaret Fox: "I found my dear wife and poor children well."

25

The King's Friend

FOUR months after Penn returned to England King Charles II was taken with an apoplexy, and in spite of all that the doctors could do—and what with bleeding him and cupping him and plying his head "with red-hot frying pans," they could do quite a lot—on February 6, 1685, he died. At three o'clock in the afternoon of that same day the Duke of York was proclaimed King James II, promising to maintain the church and state and private property and to rule with kindness.

William Penn's old friend, who had been his father's friend first, was King of England! Twenty-four years ago, riding in his brother's coronation procession, he had looked up and bowed to Admiral Penn in the flag-maker's window; twenty years ago young William Penn had taken dispatches from the Duke of York fighting the Dutch in the North Sea to King Charles at Whitehall; fifteen years ago Sir William Penn had sent his dying request to the Duke to have a care for his Quaker son, and the Duke had sent back his promise. More than once in those fifteen years the Duke had kept that promise. Vividly William Penn remembered that interview in '74 when the Duke had referred to his friendship

for the Admiral, and had said: "I am against all persecution for the sake of religion." And now James, Duke
of York, was James II, King of England.

Was this not, perhaps, an opportunity for William
Penn to help to establish, once and for all in England,
the principle of religious liberty? Had he perhaps, in returning from America just at this time, had a "leading"
to do an even more important work than settling the
boundary lines of Pennsylvania?

There were more than fourteen hundred Quakers in
prison in England at that very moment. William Penn
went to court.

He took lodgings in Charing Cross within easy walking distance of Whitehall, and every day he was at the
palace with the King. There was a genuine friendship between those two, though outsiders—both courtiers and
Quakers—found that hard to believe. They were so
different: James in his satins and laces and embroideries,
with his long narrow face, his secret reserves, his in-
flexible belief in the divine right of kings to have their
own way; and William Penn in his plain Quaker clothes
and broad hat, tall, handsome, a little portly now, with
his forthright ways, his genial friendliness, and his belief in the divine spark in every man. But James realized
that among the ambitious and self-seeking men who
thronged his court, Penn was the only man who was
sincere and unselfish—and, what in some ways was
even more remarkable, interesting and amusing as well.
He loved Penn as a "singular and entire friend," and

Penn, who for years had had reason to be grateful to James, responded with warm affection. And as always when he liked anyone, he trusted him wholly. So it was that they spent "not one but many hours together" in private, and the peers who were kept waiting in ante-rooms to see the King grew restive and jealous.

Promptly after he became King, James declared him-self a Roman Catholic, and he and his Queen went openly to mass. Penn wrote to his steward at Pennsbury Manor: "He said he concealed himself to obey his brother, and that now he would be aboveboard; which we like the better on many accounts. I was with him and told him so." But though the Friends, who concealed nothing, felt that it was better for the King to be a Papist openly than secretly, the rest of the country was thrown into panic lest he should try to establish Roman Catholicism as the state religion. People began to murmur and whisper, and to suspect everyone who was close to the King of designs against the Church of Eng-land. The old story was revived that William Penn was actually a Jesuit—more, that he was really Father Penn, a priest who had had a dispensation from the Pope to marry!

Penn, paying no attention at first to such rumors, went on with the work he had to do: the attempt to bring religious liberty to England, and the settling of his boundary dispute in America. One thing after another held him up: the election of a new Parliament, the coro-nation, the rebellion of the Duke of Monmouth against the King, which was quickly put down but not without causing much excitement and distracting the minds of everybody in power.

After the Monmouth rebellion was over, all who had taken part in it were cruelly punished; not only the leaders, but the rank and file of common people who had got into it without really knowing what it was about. Judge Jeffreys (who was the son-in-law of Sir Thomas Bludworth, one of Penn's judges in the trial of 1670) was Chief Justice, and he carried on the trial with such appalling harshness and injustice that ever afterwards the proceedings were known as the "bloody assizes." Penn went to the King and begged for mercy for the victims, but James said that the matter was in Jeffreys's hands and he could not interfere. Later, though, he rewarded Jeffreys by making him Lord Chancellor, which should have given Penn some warning about the character of his royal friend.

In October Penn and Lord Baltimore at last got a hearing for their boundary problem, and part of it at least was settled. That is, the Delaware Territories were divided by a straight line down the middle; half on the Delaware was given to Penn, and the half on the Chesapeake (now the "eastern shore" of Maryland) to Lord Baltimore. The line between Pennsylvania and Maryland, however, was not settled till years after Lord Baltimore and William Penn were both gone and two "ingenious mathematicians," Charles Mason and Jeremiah Dixon, went out from England in 1762 and drew the famous "Mason and Dixon line."

Part of his work thus, rather unsatisfactorily, done, Penn threw himself into the struggle against persecution. He presented to the King an address setting forth the sufferings of the Quakers; he wrote a tract called "A Persuasive to Moderation" in which he summoned examples from all history to back his arguments, and he pleaded untiringly for individuals. It was not only Quakers that he got released, but religious prisoners of all sects and classes. For his old friend, John Locke, who had been in exile in Holland since Sidney was executed, he got a pardon from the King. Locke, though grateful, refused to accept it, saying that he had committed no crime and therefore did not need a pardon. John Trenchard, however, a friend of a friend of his, not only accepted the pardon which Penn procured for him, but returned to England, was made chief justice of Chester, and eventually had a chance to do Penn a good turn.

Now that it was known that he had influence with the King and that he used it to help people, he was beseiged. Sometimes as many as two hundred people in a single morning came to his lodgings to beg him to intercede with the King for them or for their families. Again and again he succeeded in getting a pardon for this one, a return of his confiscated estate for that one. It took most of his time, and a good deal of his money, for when there were matters to be set forth in writing or copied out, and fees to be paid, he paid these expenses out of his own pocket.

And all the time the more people he was able to help, the more suspicious and jealous people became. The more people at large distrusted King James II, the more they feared and distrusted his friend, William Penn.

In March 1686, largely because of Penn's influence, James II issued a general pardon, and all religious prisoners were released from the jails. More than thirteen hundred Friends came forth into the wind and sunshine, some of whom had been shut up for fifteen years or more for no crime but that of worshiping God in their own way.

During the summer of that same year, Penn made a trip into Holland and Germany to visit Friends there and to tell them about Germantown and the Dutch and German settlements in Pennsylvania. Princess Elizabeth was dead now, and the Quakers in Crisheim had already gone to Germantown, but he saw some others of his old friends and he arranged for William Sewel of Amsterdam to translate his "No Cross, No Crown" and his "Account of Pennsylvania" into Dutch. At the Hague, where John Locke was living, he went to the court of William of Orange on an errand of King James. William had married James's elder daughter, Mary, and as James had no sons she was heir to the throne of England. James wanted to know how she and William felt about abolishing the Test Acts. He was planning to do it, but he knew the church party in England would oppose it vigorously, and he hoped that he could get the moral support of the next heirs, who were Protestants. William, however, said cautiously that though he was in favor of religious toleration he wouldn't go so far as to abolish the Test Acts and so let Non-Conformists and Catholics sit in Parliament. This answer Penn had to bring home to James II.

Now indeed it seemed as if Penn's work in England might be done, as if he could return to Pennsylvania. Gulielma was ready to go, the children were clamoring to see the new land and the Indians, Pennsylvania needed its governor desperately. It was still too young to go by itself. The Council had been torn by quarrels and strife, so that Penn had had to write to them: "For the love of God and me and the poor country, be not so *governmentish*." Reports trickled back to England of the way things were going in Pennsylvania, and people talked and criticized, and some who were thinking of emigrating decided not to go after all. It was all very bad for the new colony.

If he had gone to Pennsylvania then he could have straightened everything out by his mere presence, his good feeling, his kindness, and his honest desire to deal fairly with everyone. But he stayed in England.

It was one of those turning-points in our lives that steal upon us unawares, that we do not know are turning-points till years afterwards when events have proved them so. Penn did not decide not to go to Pennsylvania; he simply postponed going until it was too late. "I cannot come this fall."

It was partly a matter of money. Already he had spent, on gifts to the Indians and improvements in Philadelphia, over three thousand pounds more than he had received from sales of land. People were neglecting to pay the quit-rent they had agreed upon as part of the price of their land, and he had no salary as Governor, but many expenses instead. He felt poor, and just the moving of his family and household would cost much.

But more than that, he thought that he was needed in England. In spite of the King's general pardon in the spring, the laws against Non-Conformists were still in force—he himself had been taken three times at meetings, but was released—and he wanted to get them repealed. He more than anyone else in England had the cause of religious toleration at heart, and he more than anyone else had influence with the King. When he had won freedom for all religions, then he would go to Pennsylvania. "If it be well in England it cannot be ill in Pennsylvania," he told himself and others.

It was a mistake in judgment, not a failure of character. He simply did not see the kind of man that James was; that James wanted religious toleration not because he wanted freedom for all religions but because he wanted to put his own religion, Roman Catholicism, above the others; that he believed in the divine right of kings to rule, and maneuvered secretly but incessantly to under-

mine the power of Parliament. Because William Penn
was himself sincere and open as the day, he could not
imagine that his friend might say things which he did
not mean. It was part of William Penn's greatness that
he saw the best in people first; often just by expecting
people to be fine and honest, he made them so. But sometimes he was disappointed.

He took lodgings in large and elegant Holland House,
Kensington, and moved his family there. Now he was
more than ever with the King, always pressing the cause
of religious liberty, devoted to the King and loyally kind
to his mistakes.

For James was making mistakes. In the spring of
1687, he issued a Declaration of Indulgence, in which
he suspended the laws against Non-Conformists and
abolished the Test Acts. This was a mistake because the
King had no right to set aside the laws made by Parliament. Even people who would themselves benefit by the
Declaration of Indulgence were angry, for they saw that
the King was taking to himself power that belonged only
to Parliament. Penn led a deputation of Quakers to thank
the King, but he said in his speech that he hoped the
Parliament would agree to it, and so make it certain for
later times.

Then there was the mistake of the Magdalen Fellows.
When Magdalen College, Oxford, needed a president,
the King had recommended a Papist, who was, for other
reasons besides, unsuitable. The Fellows, who had the
right to choose their president, proceeded to elect the

man they wanted. Whereupon the King, furious, declared the election invalid and proposed another man who had Popish leanings. At this stage of the affair the King went to Oxford, and Penn with him.

Penn had been on a preaching journey through the Midlands, and the King had been on a royal progress. In several places they had met—in Chester, for instance, where the King after mass in the palace had followed Penn to meeting in the tennis court. A thousand people went to the Friends' meeting that day. On the way back to London they rode into Oxford together.

It was a Saturday early in September. The church bells were ringing, the windows along the streets were decorated with green boughs, the balconies hung with tapestries. The doctors in scarlet and the squire beadles with gold chains rode out on horseback to greet the King. The townsfolk, companies of glovers and cordwainers, tailors and mercers, led by the mayor and the bailiffs, marched out on foot. On foot too came the undergraduates in their gowns.

The King wore a scarlet coat with the bright blue ribbon of the garter across his chest, and the order of the George and Star. The bells burst into a frenzy of ringing when he came, poor women in white strewed herbs before him, people shouted *"Vivat Rex"* from all the windows. And with him rode Friend William Penn, who twenty-five years before had been expelled from Oxford, and beaten by his father because of it.

There were kneelings and speeches in Latin, there

were "wind musick" and university singers; there was claret running in the conduits for the vulgar, and banquets for the great in Christ Church Hall and Bodley's library.

While he was in Oxford, the King sent for the Fellows of Magdalen and ordered them to elect his choice for president. They refused, saying they had already elected their man, and they could not go back on their oath. He threatened them with the full weight of his wrath.

Next morning they sent for Penn and discussed their plight with him, and he, seeing the justice of their case, promised to write a letter to the King for them. He did write it, but the King paid no attention to it. He did only those kind and tolerant acts that would further his own secret ends—but Penn never saw that.

The whole affair roused great indignation in England and a good deal of fear. People thought the Papists were trying to get control of the universities. One more black mark was written up against James II.

His final mistake was to repeat in the spring of 1688 his Declaration of Indulgence, and to order the ministers to read it out in all the churches. When seven Bishops refused, he clapped them into the Tower of London— and all England bubbled and seethed with righteous anger.

Penn, sincerely distressed, did what he could. Choosing the moment of all others when James would be in a happy and yielding frame of mind, the day on which his only son was born, Penn went to him and implored him in honor of this tiny Prince of Wales to set free the seven Bishops. James refused.

When the Bishops came to trial, they were acquitted, and all England rejoiced, and felt more than ever convinced that James II was not the King the country wanted.

Perhaps, after all, that poor little Prince of Wales— who years later became the father of Bonnie Prince Charlie—was James's worst mistake. So long as Protestant Mary of Orange was heir to the throne, England felt safe; but now that a boy was born, who would unquestionably be brought up a Catholic, the whole situation was changed. The strongest and most powerful among the nobility and gentry took counsel together. They wrote to William of Orange, Mary's husband, and' invited him to come to England, and bring his army with him.

He landed at Torbay in Devon with fourteen thousand men on the fifth of November 1688; the noblemen who had invited him to come joined him at once; some of the King's army deserted and went to him; and James's favorite daughter Anne took sides with her sister and brother-in-law against her father. James, overwhelmed with surprise and grief, cried out: "God help me, my own children have forsaken me!" He sent his wife and baby son to France and, after a feeble effort or two, he himself fled to join them there early in December.

The convention of nobles then proclaimed the throne vacant and crowned William and Mary as King and

Queen. The Bloodless Revolution of 1688 was accomplished.

And now William Penn, the friend of James II, was a lonely figure in England. The others who had been much at court had run away. Father Petre, James's confessor, had gone with him. Robert Spencer, the Earl of Sunderland, Penn's old friend in France, went off in his wife's cap and petticoat. Lord Jeffreys tried to escape in the dress of a common sailor, but was caught. Penn alone remained.

Pennsylvania needed him, but to go to Pennsylvania now would be to run away like the others, as if he were guilty of something, and frightened. He couldn't go now. He had to stay.

26

Hunted

A MONTH after William of Orange landed in England, William Penn, walking openly in Whitehall, was arrested and taken before the Lords of Council to be questioned. He answered honestly and fearlessly that he loved his country and the Protestant religion more than life itself and had never done anything against either, that King James had been his friend and his father's friend, and that in gratitude he was the King's friend and had always tried so far as he could to influence him for his good. James's other friends had deserted him or had fled with him; William Penn alone dared to stand before the new government and declare openly his affection for the banished King.

Though the Lords of Council could not help admiring his sincerity and loyalty, they would not let him go free till he had given bail to appear again the first day of the next term. He returned to Worminghurst and stayed there until the Easter term, when, nothing having been found against him, he was cleared by the court.

In 1689, the first year of the reign of William and Mary, that thing happened toward which Penn's strength had been bent for the last twenty years: religious liberty became a principle of law. Parliament passed the Act of Toleration and the King approved it. It was not a perfect law, for, the Test Acts still remaining in force, Non-Conformists could not sit in Parliament, hold any office in the government, or be educated at the universities; but it was the first step, and a big one, in the right direction. It provided that those who took oaths of loyalty to the present government should be exempt from the old harsh laws against Non-Conformists, and members of the Society of Friends were allowed to give their solemn promise instead of swearing. The ironic thing about it was that the man who by his writings, his speeches, his imprisonments, and the example of his government in Pennsylvania, had done more than any other one person to bring this Toleration Act into being, was completely out of favor with those who passed it, and under suspicion. William Penn had been James's friend and—some said—a Jesuit!

It mattered not a bit to Penn who got the credit; toleration had come to England. He turned his thoughts toward Pennsylvania. Captain Blackwell, whom he had sent out as deputy-governor, had proved unsatisfactory to the colony, and Penn advised him to resign. He wrote to the Council in Pennsylvania, urging them to name three or five men from whom he would choose one for governor. He wrote, too, instructing the Council to set up a public school, under the care of Friends, in which the poor were to be taught free, those who could pay for their children were to do so, and all were to be eligible to attend, Friends and non-Friends. The first master was to be his old friend, George Keith, the mathematician from the University of Aberdeen who had traveled in Holland and Germany with him in 1677. This is the school now called the William Penn Charter School.

In 1690 Penn was again arrested and brought before the Lords of Council, this time on the charge of corresponding with the former King. He asked to be taken before King William himself.

A letter was brought out written by James to Penn. "Mr. Penn, why did the late King James write to you?"

"I know not," Penn replied. "But it is impossible for me to prevent the King from writing to me if he choose to do so. I confess freely, however, that I loved King James—and if I loved him in his prosperity I cannot now hate him in his adversity. But I have never so much as thought of trying to restore to him the crown which has fallen from his head—and so nothing in that letter can in any way bring guilt on me."

Anyone who had studied character would know that he could count on the loyalty and integrity of a man who could speak like that. King William knew it, and was ready to set Penn free at once, but some of his Council preferred to look upon this loyal and generous speech as a "barefaced espousing of King James's cause," and so, giving in to them, William ordered Penn to give bail to appear at the next Trinity term. When that came, he was again honorably discharged.

Now, drawing a long breath, he began to prepare to
go to Pennsylvania—and immediately fresh turmoil
arose. James, with French troops to support him, landed
in Ireland, and the Irish joined with him in rebellion.
The French fleet sailed into English waters and attacked the English Navy. "Europe looks like a sea of
trouble," Penn had written a year earlier, and now indeed the trouble had come. King William went to Ireland with an army, and Queen Mary, left in command at
home, nervously arrested eighteen men who she feared
might raise a rebellion for James in England. One of the
eighteen was William Penn. Once again he was brought
to trial, and once again they could find nothing against
him.

Set free, he went on with his plans. He published proposals for a second settlement in Pennsylvania, this one
to be in that territory along the Susquehanna River
which he himself had explored. He made all his arrangements to go himself, even to getting from the Secretary
of State an order for a convoy, since a little merchant
vessel could not venture unprotected into a sea so full of
French warships. Now everything was set.

On the thirteenth of January 1691, dear George Fox
died, in a house near Gracechurch Street meeting. Penn
was with him, and almost his last words were: "William,
mind poor friends in America."

"A prince indeed is fallen in Israel," wrote Penn to
Margaret Fox in Lancashire. Hardship had fallen upon

the Friends before, but this was an irreparable loss, and a keen personal grief as well, for Fox was known to each and every one and loved by all.

By the hundreds they came to his funeral at Bunhill Fields to pay him their last service of honor and devotion. Penn spoke to the multitude there—and just escaped being taken by officers who had been sent to arrest him and arrived too late.

He soon heard about it. A warrant was out against him. A man named William Fuller (who later was declared by Parliament to be "a cheat and a notorious impostor") had sworn on his oath that Penn and others had conspired against the government. Treason was the ugly charge against him.

The ship was ready to sail for Pennsylvania. It sailed without Penn and his family.

If he escaped to Pennsylvania with a warrant out for his arrest in England, his enemies would hail it as an admission of guilt. If he gave himself up, he would be faced in court by this Fuller who would swear to his lies, while Penn who spoke the truth could not speak it on oath. Even if he were acquitted, he was likely to be arrested again. Three times in the last two years had he been arrested, and acquitted.

Feeling "hunted up and down," he took lodgings in London on a little street off the Strand, and there in hiding he waited for the storm to pass over his head.

Gulielma and the children stayed at Worminghurst, though now and then she came up to visit a friend at

Hoddesdon, near London, from where she could slip into the city and visit her William in his hiding-place. She was forty-seven now, and the anxieties and troubles of the last few years made her seem older than she was. That William Penn, who had been governor of a province in America, the friend of a king, the champion of liberty, and was besides the finest and most charming of men, should be hiding in a little house with a peep-hole in the door and a secret way of escape by the river, all but broke her proud and loving heart. Her courage failed her, not for herself but for him, and her health, never robust, wasted away.

Others besides Gulielma came to see William Penn in his retirement: Henry Sidney, Algernon's brother, and John Locke, who had come from the Hague with William and Mary, and was high in their favor. He offered to get a pardon for Penn from the King, but Penn, like Locke himself only a few years before when Penn was up on the political seesaw and Locke was down, refused it on the grounds that being innocent, he could not be pardoned.

Bad news came from Pennsylvania. The Province and the Territories were quarreling over the choice of deputy-governor, and the Society of Friends itself was torn by a dispute about religious beliefs which George Keith had started. And Penn had been so certain that if only people were given religious liberty, peace and unity must follow! He was distressed and disappointed, and tied here as he was, all he could do for his people was to write them letters.

Worse than either of these matters, though trouble-some as they were, was the final, the shattering blow, which fell in the summer of 1692. The King took Pennsylvania away from Penn and put it under the rule of Governor Fletcher of New York.

Trouble indeed. His enemies were complacent, his friends had turned aside from him, people whom he had helped in their troubles forgot him in his. He was declared a traitor in Ireland, and Shangarry forfeited to the Crown. Worst of all, his beloved Pennsylvania, which he had built with such high hopes, such loving forethought and which had made him poor, now was taken from him. His life had touched its lowest point.

But William Penn was not the man to sit down with despair—not so long as he could put pen to paper and the ink held out. He wrote letters to the Society of Friends, to the influential noblemen whom he knew, to Pennsylvania. In spite of having lost the government there he still hoped to go to America, if he could get the King's permission.

Even in the midst of his own pressing wrongs, Penn could look beyond his own concerns and see the problems of the world. His "Essay towards the Present and Future Peace of Europe," published in 1693, proposed a league of nations in Europe over two hundred years before the world got around to trying out the idea. His other great work of this period he called "Some Fruits of Solitude," and published anonymously. It was a little book of "reflections and maxims," relating to the conduct of human life, and into it he put a great deal of "honest, kindly wisdom" (as Robert Louis Stevenson said of it), simply and sometimes beautifully expressed. It is good reading for thoughtful people today.

"There can be no friendship," he wrote, "where there is no freedom. Friendship loves a free air, and will not be penned up in straight and narrow enclosures. It will speak freely, and act so too; and take nothing ill where no ill is meant. . . . A true friend unbosoms freely, advises justly, assists readily, adventures boldly, takes all patiently, defends courageously, and continues a friend unchangeably. . . . Choose a friend as thou dost a wife, till death separate you."

So he was occupied in this period of retirement. All things come to an end. "This too will pass," the old minstrel sang in the days when the English suffered from the invading Danes. At the close of 1693, Penn's friends at court, Henry Sidney, who was now Lord Romney, Lord Hyde, now Lord Rochester, and Lord Ranelagh, went to the King and asked for Penn's release. They had known him, they said, some of them for thirty years (that would be Henry Sidney) and had never known him to do an ill thing, but on the contrary many good ones. The King replied that Penn was an old acquaintance of his too, and that he might follow his business as freely as ever, and he promised to say the same to the Secretary of State, Sir John Trenchard. It was the same Jack Trenchard whom Penn had taken in his coach to Windsor Castle to be pardoned by King James; after the

Revolution Trenchard had bought from Penn the four horses that had drawn the coach that day. And now Penn, on the thirtieth of November, went to Sir John Trenchard to receive his official exoneration—not pardon.

With him went his eldest son, Springett, a tall boy of seventeen now, more like his mother than ever, with his gentle seriousness and his fine mind, a companion and a joy to his father. Coming away from Sir John's, they went to the Friends' meeting at the Bull and Mouth, stopped in at Penn's lodgings in the Strand ("the sanctuary of my solitude") for a last errand, and from there went straight to Hoddesdon, where Gulielma and Tishe and Billy were.

As soon as he saw Guli, Penn knew that she was really ill; but as her illness had been caused by her intense anxiety for him, he hoped that his safe return and the joyful reunion of the family would cure it. But happiness came too late. They had two months together, and then, on February 23, 1694, "in great sweetness and peace she departed."

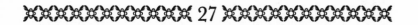

27

Hannah

SPRINGETT was eighteen now, a delicate boy, and very serious-minded, inclined to look on games and sports and pleasures as "sad stuff." For a time he had been in Amsterdam studying with William Sewel; and even after he came home again he went on exchanging letters in Latin with that learned gentleman. Because of his character and his interests he, more than either of the others, was his father's friend and companion. Tishe, sixteen, and Billy, fourteen, lively and energetic, squirmed a little under their elder brother's admonitions, and privately considered, though they did not say so aloud, that as a family the Penns had suffered a good deal more for their Quakerism than was desirable.

With Gulielma gone, life at Worminghurst was sad and disorganized. Penn could not endure to stay there for long at a time now—and besides his affairs called him away. But he worried about his children, so young, so restless, so terribly in need of a mother.

He himself was busy about the affairs of Pennsylvania, and with his writing. Thomas Ellwood had edited George Fox's *Journal*, and Penn had been asked to write a preface to it. It was for him a labor of love, and instead of dashing off page after page, without blotting it, as he usually did, he wrote slowly and with care, pruning and revising. When it was finished, he had written not only an account of George Fox full of love and insight, but a history of Quakerism and its origins. The London Monthly Meeting approved what he had written, but unfortunately Margaret Fox, influenced by two of her sons-in-law, Thomas Lower and William Mead, who had criticized Penn severely for his activities at court in the time of James II, refused to allow it to be published with the *Journal*. Printed separately with the title "The Rise and Progress of the People Called Quakers," it went into several editions.

Everybody seemed glad to welcome him back into the sunlight. Wherever he went, people flocked to hear him speak, so that sometimes there would be too many for the hall or the market-house and he would have to go out into the nearest field.

In August 1694, Pennsylvania was returned to him. Governor Fletcher of New York had tried to govern it as he ruled the army, and had not been successful. The colony, thankful to be back under Penn's rule, was in a mood to be much less "governmentish" than it had once been. William Markham, Penn's cousin, was once again deputy-governor over the Province and the Territories, and George Keith, who had stirred up so much strife in Philadelphia, now returned to England. Though he became an Episcopal minister and wrote tracts against both Quakerism and Penn, he was much less disturbing there than he had been in Pennsylvania. The colony settled down to a period of peace and prosperity, and Philadelphia grew so fast that the city of New York was dismayed.

The last four months of the year Penn spent in and about Bristol. When he came home to Worminghurst, he had a great deal to say about Hannah Callowhill. The children had known her slightly, for she was the daughter and the granddaughter of prominent Friends in Bristol, and they liked her. She was brisk and practical but sweet-tempered; she had downright kindly ways that made people feel comfortable with her; she had a sort of restful, undemanding charm that made people forget that she was thirty and unmarried and homely. After Tishe had had Hannah Callowhill held up to her a few times by her father as an example, and had seen his pleasure in talking of Hannah, she "perceived which way his inclination was taking." But she kept it to herself. She was content.

William Penn never did anything by halves. He was fifty-one, and he had had great contrasts in his life: he had had the world in his hands and he had put it aside to become a Quaker in a day when to be a Quaker meant ridicule and scorn and persecution; he had been in prison with the lowest and he had walked with the King as a friend; he had owned a great province and lost it and got it again; he had known victory and defeat, failure and success, great happiness and great sorrow. Into every experience as it came to him he had entered fully; nothing that was in his life had he ever evaded at the time or repudiated afterwards. He rarely looked back. Instead, he strode forward to meet the future with zest and a rare freshness of spirit. He loved Hannah Callowhill, and he courted her ardently. In June he sent her the Earl of Leicester's recipe for dried apples; by September he was writing to her:

"Most deare Hannah Callowhill:

"I would perswade myself thou art of the same minde, tho it is hard to make thee say so. Yet it must come in time, I hope and believe, for why should I love so well and so much where I am not well beloved? . . .

"Thy unchangeable friend, W.P."

She made him stay away for two months while she made up her mind, but in November he was in Bristol again, and on the eleventh they declared their intention of marriage to the Monthly Meeting.

From Bristol he went to Wells to preach. Though the Bishop had given him permission to speak in the market-house, Friends arriving there were forbidden by the clerk to go in. Accordingly they went to the Crown Inn across the way, an old building with a little oaken gallery overlooking the market-place. There Penn stood and preached to the two or three thousand people who crowded together in the street below. Beyond the sea of faces lifted up to him, the great cathedral towered into the air, and the ancient gateway known as the Bishop's Eye glowered on the scene.

In the middle of his "declaration" a constable bustled up with a warrant from the Mayor, and once again William Penn was arrested and dragged away. This time he could prove that his meeting had been certified by the Bishop, and the Mayor, realizing that he had disturbed a lawful assembly, was sufficiently abashed to apologize.

From Wells, Penn went back to Worminghurst to take care of Springett, who had "an ugly cold and cough." Every day or two he wrote to his dearest Hannah.

"My poor Boy is better, and in a way, I hope, of recovery, often pert and projecting his journey to London and Bristol. . . . Remember ever that I am, with the greatest truth and best of love,

"Thyn from all the world, William Penn."

Hannah on the contrary, was not, it seems, a very prolific letter-writer.

"This is my eighth letter to thy fourth since I saw thee," wrote W.P. reproachfully. And later:

"This is my tenth letter to thy fourth, which is a disproportion I might begin to reproach thee for, but I do it so gently and with so much affection that I hope it will prevail with thee to mend thy pace."

And another time: "I cannot forbear to write where I cannot forbear to love."

In February 1696 he wrote: "Count of me, thyself, as

the man of the world that most entirely loves and values thee above every other sincere comfort and therefore is, with great delight, thyn as he ought to be, W.P."

A few days later, he was writing to his "dearest and best-beloved friend" about his plans for the trip to Bristol and the wedding. On the twenty-fourth of the month, the meeting in Bristol gave them leave to proceed, and at once William Penn and Springett, who had not got rid of his cough, Letitia, and Billy, set forth from Worminghurst for Bristol.

William Penn and Hannah Callowhill were married on the fifth of March 1696 at Friars Meeting-House. Hannah's father, Thomas Callowhill, and her grandfather, Dennis Hollister, were there, both solid, well-thought-of Bristol merchants; Penn's three children were there; and a host of Friends and friends besides. It was a "weighty" meeting. So many of the early leaders of the Friends were gone: dear George Fox, Isaac and Mary Penington, Robert Barclay, and those ardent First Publishers of Truth who went out two by two in the '50s. Of these valiant ones, William Penn alone was left, but he was young at fifty-one.

28

Back to Pennsylvania

AFTER Springett, that dear "companion and friend," died, the Penns left Worminghurst and moved to Bristol. They both loved the little city that struggled to be a second and better London. It was Hannah's home, and William Penn had known it almost all his life. He knew the quays where the ships came up among the houses of the town; in Redcliffe steeplehouse hung his father's armor and the flags of his squadrons; he had ridden out through Lawford's Gate with Josiah Coale and down the London Road; he and Guli had met George and Margaret Fox at the Fair in St. James's churchyard. He had walked with Hannah along the banks of the Frome; they had been married in Friars Meeting-House.

Tishe and Billy were contented here. Billy was smitten with a little Quakeress named Mary Jones, and his father hoped that she, being four years older, might have a steadying influence on him. He felt uneasy about Billy, he was so fierce of temper and so weak of will, so easily led by his affections, and so quickly alienated, so eager for the things of the world. When in 1698 he had to go to Ireland, he took Billy, then seventeen, and Thomas Story with him.

Thomas Story was a well-educated young man who had been a Friend for about seven years. William Penn had met him the year before in London and had taken a liking to him. He and another young Friend, learning that the youthful Czar of Russia, later to be known as Peter the Great, was staying in Mr. Evelyn's house in Deptford and learning shipbuilding at the shipyards there, had gone to see him and tried to convince him of Quakerism. As they could not speak German and the Czar could not speak English or read the Latin of Barclay's *Apology*, which they presented him with, they did not make much headway. William Penn and George Whitehead followed them in a few days, talked to the Czar in German and gave him Quaker books that had been translated into German. Though Peter the Great never became a Quaker—he felt that there was something fundamentally inconvenient about a religion that forbade war—still he did go to meeting at Deptford, and fifteen years later he was still enough impressed by Quakerism to say: "Whoever could live according to that doctrine would be happy." Remembering this episode, Penn wrote to Thomas Story from Bristol and asked him to meet him at Holyhead in Wales, to go to Ireland.

It was nearly thirty years since Penn had been in Ireland. Many things there were just as he had always known them. Shangarry was his again, having been returned to him minus several years' rent. Ireland, as before, was suffering from the effects of war and invasion; the campaign of the Boyne, in which King William had driven out James and punished his supporters, had laid waste that green land once again and written misery and grief upon the faces of the poor in the cottages. Troopers went about taking horses from Papists and from Quakers, who could not swear they were not Papists. Quaker meetings were still likely to be invaded by magistrates and constables. Lord Shannon alone of all the great ones whom Penn had known before was still there—but now, though he was still glad for his friendship, Penn no longer needed his protection. The Mayors of Cork and Dublin were respectful, the Bishops were friendly, and the Lords Justices of Ireland were ready to frown on anybody who dared to be otherwise.

They spent three months there in the spring of '98, mostly in Dublin and Cork, and everywhere that William Penn went people crowded to hear him preach. The Dean of Derry went several times, and reported to his Bishop that "his heart said amen to what he heard"; at Cashel the Bishop complained that when he went to church to preach nobody was there but the Mayor and the churchwardens and a few constables, all the rest of his congregation having gone to hear Penn. When some cocky young officers ordered their dragoons to confiscate Penn's horse at the ferry near Waterford, they found themselves in very hot water afterwards, and in great perturbation they appealed to Penn to intercede for them with the authorities. Which he, who bore a grudge to no one, least of all young scamps like these, did to such effect that they were immediately released and forgiven.

By the middle of August they were back in Bristol again, where Thomas Story stayed for several weeks with the Penns before he set forth for America. Penn, delighted that he was going, went all the way to London to see him off. He was glad to have such men as Thomas Story in Pennsylvania.

Another young man whom Penn picked out for Pennsylvania was James Logan. He was a Friend by birth, the son of Scottish parents who had gone to live in Ireland when their estates in Scotland were confiscated. For some years now his father had been master in the Friends' school that was held in the upper room of Friars Meeting-House in Bristol, and for a time James, who knew Latin and Greek and Hebrew at thirteen, taught himself mathematics at sixteen, and picked up French and Italian and some Spanish in odd moments, had been his assistant. When William Penn first knew him, he was engaged in trade between Bristol and Dublin, a tall, fine-looking young man of twenty-five, full of courage and determination and loyalty and a certain Highland hot-headedness. Penn, who made so many mistakes in his judgment of character, made none when he put his trust in James Logan. When in the summer of 1699, he was ready at last to go to Pennsylvania he asked Logan to go with him as his secretary, and Logan—to Pennsylvania's great good fortune—agreed.

It took a bit of maneuvering to get ready. Funds were low. He had given Worminghurst to Billy when that young man insisted—barely eighteen he was!—on marrying his Mary Jones on the twelfth of January 1699. And besides, he was poor on Pennsylvania's account. The people would not pay their quit-rents. He had, with rash generosity, refused to have a tax levied for his benefit in 1683, and now the Council would not impose one to pay the expenses of government—the deputy-governor, the assemblies, the costs of the boundary adjustments—all of which fell on William Penn. Then there had been the gifts to the Indians, the cost of surveying land, and the bills and bills and bills for the house at Pennsbury Manor. In the end he borrowed money from his agent, Philip Ford, of Bristol. For years now Ford had been his man of business and knew so much more about his financial affairs than Penn did that he signed the legal papers Ford prepared without even reading them. A most dangerous thing to do.

On September 7, 1699, they sailed from Cowes on the Isle of Wight—William Penn and Hannah and Tishe and James Logan. Billy refused to go with them. He and his Mary would rather stay in England, thank you. So Penn, having given them Worminghurst, gathered up the advice and guidance that Billy was too impatient to listen to, wrote it all down in a little book that he called *Fruits of a Father's Love,* and left it with him to read, if he would. It wasn't much, he thought with misgiving, but it was the most he could do at present. Springett had been the one like Guli, the one that Mary Penington had been fondest of; Billy had always been difficult. It worried him to leave Billy now, but there was Pennsylvania—also his child—needing him desperately too, and, as Billy did not, asking for his help and his presence.

This time the crossing took three months. It was December, and a particularly cold and raw December, before, battered and ice-coated, the little ship *Canterbury* dropped anchor in the Delaware near Chester, late one gray afternoon. Penn, impulsive at fifty-five as he had been at thirty-three, could not endure the thought of spending another night on the ship when he might be on land. He had the little boat let down and had a sailor row him up the creek. This time there were no city gates for him to find shut tight for the night. Thomas Story was waiting eagerly to welcome him at Lydia Wade's house.

Story had traveled all over the American colonies, from North Carolina to Massachusetts and back to Philadelphia. He had much to tell Penn. It was just as well the voyage had taken as long as it did—yellow fever had been raging in Philadelphia. For a while five or six people a week had died (did Penn think of the Great Plague in London when seven thousand had died in a week?), but now it was over and people, though saddened, were pulling themselves together again. They talked late, sitting in high-backed walnut chairs within the great stone fireplace. The younger man was filled with joy at having his hero and friend safe at last in his own province, and Penn, eternally young at heart, was glad in Thomas's companionship. If only Billy . . .

The next morning the Governor made his official entrance into Pennsylvania with all ceremony, and the whole town of Chester was out to welcome him. One sad thing happened. Chester possessed two rusty old sea-pieces of cannon left over from the days of the Dutch, and some young irrepressibles, who had been expressly forbidden to do so by the Mayor, fired off a salute in his honor. The first round went off in fine style, the little guns recoiled and boomed most satisfactorily; but the second time, one of the boys, named B. Bevan, threw in a cartridge of powder before the piece was sponged—and his arm exploded with the cannon. Joy turned to consternation, and Penn was filled with distress. He did not forget the incident as the days went on, crowded with affairs, but continued to pay for Bevan's relief, support, and surgical aid, until in April there was one last, sad bill to pay.

After the greetings in Chester, Penn returned to the ship, and they sailed up the river to Philadelphia. Tishe and Hannah Penn wrapped in furs were out on deck in the "dry, wild, piercing, and hungry air," that stung their cheeks and froze their breath. Indians, their feathers blowing, came out in canoes to greet them, townspeople crowded to the waterside.

Philadelphia had grown. There were four hundred houses now, of wood and stone and brick, built along the straight wide streets. Smoke from their chimneys mounted straight up and the smell of it was pleasantly tangy in the nostrils. The steeple of the Episcopal church gleamed white against the wintry blue sky. But the trees! Where were the trees?

Even while he met the crowd that had gathered to welcome him, greeting old friends with hearty affection and meeting the new men who had risen to importance in the town, Penn saw that the trees were gone. Ruthlessly, recklessly, they had cut down the trees to build their houses and to keep them warm. The trees of his green country town. . . .

From the landing he went first to make a call of state upon the deputy-governor, his cousin William Markham, and from there, for it was the first day of the week, to the big meeting-house at Fourth and Mulberry Streets. In the silence he found peace and hope and fellowship and an inexpressible lifting of the spirit. Again and again Pennsylvania was to hurt him, but always he would find healing in meeting.

For the first month they stayed with Edward Shippen, and after that they moved into the house that Samuel Carpenter had vacated for them. It stood on Second Street between Chestnut and Walnut, at the corner of Norris's Alley, a plain comfortable stone building known as "the slate-roofed house."

There was no mistaking the joy with which Pennsylvania received its Governor and his family. James Logan wrote to William Junior about it: "Friends' love to the Governor was great and sincere; they had long mourned for his absence and passionately desired his return. He,

Penn's home in Philadelphia

they firmly believed, would compose all their difficulties and repair all that was amiss."

The slate-roofed house was warm and comfortable, and everybody was ready with a thousand kindnesses: Friends and church people, and Indians with their gifts of venison and wild turkey for their beloved Onas. Within doors were firelight and candlelight, polished furniture, good food and good wine, good talk. Men came to talk with Penn about government and meeting matters, about distant places, and books. Francis Daniel Pastorius, who was now teaching at the Friends' School around the corner, came in often; and Thomas Story, Samuel Carpenter, Edward Shippen, Isaac Norris. James Logan was always there. For Hannah Penn there were gentle women with whispers of encouragement and help, and around Tishe, pretty, twenty-year-old Tishe in her lavender silk from London, the young people came flocking, girls in Quaker gray—she gave a doll she had brought with her from England to one very little girl and laughed to see her eyes widen in wonder and in joy —and very shy, very reverent young men. One of them, young William Masters, was soon very adoring too. James Logan preferred to talk to the Governor; perhaps he had seen enough of Tishe in those three months on the *Canterbury*.

Inside the slate-roofed house all was warmth and friendliness. Outside, there was the wind whistling and howling in a way it didn't in Bristol to remind them that miles of winter fields "like blocks of ice, and the woods as if candied" closed in on them, and that three months of tossing ocean lay between them and England. William Penn exulted in it, but Hannah Penn and Tishe carried fear like a little cold fish deep under the layers of other things in their hearts.

At the end of January a new baby was born, the only little American in the family. John, they called him, and even from the first he was a "comely lively babe, who has much of his father's grace and air."

The Friends' school boys proceeded to celebrate the event with a poem:

"To William Penn, the Father of this Province and lately also the Father of John Penn, an innocent and hopeful babe:

"Since children are the Lord's reward,
  Who get them may rejoice;
Nay, neighbors, upon this regard,
  May make a gladsome noise.

"Therefore, we think we dwell so near,
  Dear Governor, to thy Gate,
That thou mayest lend an ear to hear
  What Babes congratulate.

"God bless the child (we young ones cry)
  And add from time to time
To William Penn's Posterity
  The Like! Here ends our Rime.

"But fervent prayers will not end
  Of honest men for thee
And for the happy government
  With whom we all agree."

He was just a little more than two months younger
than his niece Gulielma Maria, who had been born at
Worminghurst in November while the *Canterbury* was
still tossing in mid-ocean.

29

Pennsbury Manor

IN THE spring they moved to Pennsbury Manor. For fifteen years it had been getting ready for them. The first front door, which was too low and mean, had been replaced by a better one sent out from England. The gardener, Hugh Sharp, with three Negroes under him, had planted the walnuts, hawthorns, hazels, and cherry trees sent out from Worminghurst, and the shrubs and plants from Maryland, and had transplanted wild flowers from the forests. Around the house were flower gardens and wide lawns; from the upper terrace steps led to an avenue lined with poplars that stretched down to the Delaware; vistas cut through the trees to left and right showed the encircling river.

When they sailed up to it in the barge, they saw the big brick house at the end of its poplar walk, surrounded by a cloud of cherry trees in bloom. The oak pillars of the porch, brought from England, were carved with vines and grapes. A generous and substantial house it was, simple yet gracious, fitting for the Governor of a great, young province.

Inside, the great hall stretched the full length of the house, with a long oak table and benches, pewter plates and dishes, for council meetings, the Governor pointed out, and for entertaining Indians and strangers. The little hall, for smaller groups, had leather chairs and five maps hung upon the walls. (How long ago young William Penn had gone with Mr. Pepys to the booksellers' in St. Paul's churchyard to pick out prints and maps!) On the other side of the hall were three parlors wainscoted in walnut, elegantly furnished with chairs cushioned in satin, with spider tables, Penn's own great leather armchair, a clock, and brasses for the fireplaces. Upstairs the best bedroom had satin curtains and cushions and a satin bedspread, the other three had striped linen and camlet. In the attic there were four beds for overflow.

Behind the house, built like it and set out in a straight line, were the outhouses: the kitchen and larder, the wash-house, the bake-house and brew-house, the stable for twelve horses. There were a coach and a light carriage called a calash, three sidesaddles and two pillions. The sedan chair had been brought up from Philadelphia too, but there would not be much use for it here in the country; even the coach and calash would not be nearly so comfortable on these deep-rutted bumpy roads as the sidesaddles.

And then Penn had his barge, which he loved "above all dead things." All his seafaring blood boiled up to the surface as he fussed over this boat which was all his own. It became well known on the Delaware. Once when Samuel Jennings of Burlington, across the river in New Jersey, and some friends were having a comfortable smoke, they saw Penn's barge heave into sight, and quickly, for they knew his dislike of tobacco, they hid their pipes. He came upon them, though, before the smoke, or the smell of it, had entirely vanished, and said jokingly: "Well, gentlemen, I am glad you have sufficient grace to be ashamed of the practice!" To which Samuel Jennings replied blandly: "Oh, no, not ashamed at all. We simply desisted in order to avoid hurting a weak brother"—and they all laughed heartily.

The Penns spent the greater part of the year at Pennsbury Manor, returning to the slate-roofed house only for the coldest part of the winter. Penn was often called away. Off he would go, riding his great horse Tamerlane, or sailing in his barge. He went to see Lord Baltimore and took him and his wife, at their request, to a Friends' meeting. They arrived late, however, when meeting was almost over, and Lady Baltimore was disappointed not to have heard a "husbandman or a shoemaker or such-like rustic" inspired to speak. "I do not wish to hear you speak," she complained to Penn. "I do not question that you can do it, for you are a scholar and a wise man, but I should not expect these others to preach to any purpose."

"Some of them are rather the best preachers we have among us," returned Penn mildly.

He rode to Conestoga, where he stayed with the Indian king in his "palace," and came home across the Schuylkill River. He rode to Friends' meetings all through the Welsh Tract. One Sunday morning, on his way to Haverford, he overtook a little girl plodding by herself along the road from Darby. He drew up his horse.

"My child, where art thou going?"

"To the meeting at Haverford, sir, where the Governor is to be."

"Then climb up behind me. There is little to be gained by walking when it is possible to ride!"

They found a stump that she could climb upon, and from there she scrambled up behind him; so, with her small arms clasped around the Governor's waist and her bare legs dangling over the side of the Governor's horse, Rebecca Wood went to meeting.

But while the Governor rode abroad, his wife and daughter stayed at Pennsbury. Now and then they went to an Indian cantico. Now and then company came up from Philadelphia. More often a farm woman from the neighborhood came in with country produce to sell and found the Governor's wife, "a delicate, pretty woman," sitting beside the cradle of her baby. There was not even that usual feminine solace, shopping. They had to write to Philadelphia for the things they needed: a flitch of bacon, chocolate and coffee-berries, earthen pans for milking and baking, Indian meal, linen for towels, frieze for the servants' clothes, wick for candles, barrels for cider.

Among the servants there had been three slaves to work in the garden, but in 1701 Penn set them free. Slave-holding had slipped into Pennsylvania in spite of the protest which Pastorius and the Germantown Quakers had made against it in 1688. Penn felt a great concern for the slaves; he persuaded the Council to pass a bill to regularize their marriages, but the Assembly threw it out. Many Friends freed their slaves, as he did, and provided for their start in life, but it was not till eighty years later that the Society of Friends as a whole took a stand against slave-holding.

All was not smooth sailing for the Governor in this province that had so passionately longed for his coming "to compose all their difficulties and repair everything that was amiss." He found his people harder to deal with than he had thought. When they wished to change the Charter, he said to them: "Friends, if in the constitution by charter there be anything that jars, alter it. If you want a law for this or that, prepare it." He made all the members of the Council into a committee to "read the Charter and Frame of Government, to keep what is good in either, to lay aside what is inconvenient or burdensome, and to add to both what may best suit the common good." But they could not agree on the changes. There was constant friction between the Province and the Territories, and there was a good deal of grumbling and complaining on all sides.

Penn felt hurt by all of this. He had lost more than twenty thousand pounds on Pennsylvania by this time, and he felt that in all things he had tried to deal generously with the people. But they had managed to "cut collops" out of his acres at Pennsbury Manor, they resented being taxed to pay for the costs of government, they insisted that he ought to sell his land at the original price, though values had increased and they were selling their land for much more than they paid him for it. Penn, like many generous people, loved to give but hated to be imposed upon. It seemed to him sometimes that his people were being ungrateful and unreasonable.

On the colonists' side there was this to be said: there were two distinct parties in Pennsylvania now, the Quakers and the Church party, centering about Christ Church. They had equal numbers and equal political rights, but they had different ideas and there were inevitable disagreements. Then, though they had freedom to make their own laws, they had it as the gift of the proprietor, Penn. That was all right when he himself was there; they trusted his justice and generosity, and were soothed by his tact in dealing with people; but they did not always like the deputy-governors he sent to take his place when he was away, and they were anxious about the future when his children would inherit his power in Pennsylvania. They wanted a constitution that would make them safe—and they had different ideas about what that constitution should be.

In the summer of 1701 word came from England that certain people in Parliament were trying to put through a bill that would take all the proprietary governments away from their proprietors or owners, and give them to the Crown to rule. New Jersey, Pennsylvania, Maryland, Virginia, and South Carolina were the proprietary governments in America, but none of them would be so hard hit by the change as Pennsylvania. None of the others, except New Jersey, had so much freedom to lose, and New Jersey, having found twenty-four proprietors at least twenty too many, welcomed the idea of being handed over to the Crown. Pennsylvania was the only one of the colonies that had no militia, no forts, no cannon; its policy of peace had been successful with the Indians; not a single white man had been killed by Indians in Pennsylvania, though all the other colonies had suffered terrible and terrifying massacres. If Pennsylvania were annexed by the Crown, she would be taxed to maintain a militia which she did not want and which might destroy all her good relations with the Indians. Penn's friends in England urged him to come home and to appear in Parliament to defend his rights.

He had to go. But he would stay only till he got his business done, and then come back. He wanted to leave his family to wait for him in Pennsylvania, but they would have nothing to do with such an idea. With an air of surprise he wrote from Pennsbury to James Logan in Philadelphia: "I cannot prevail on my wife to stay; still less Tishe." But Hannah promised that when he was ready to return to Pennsylvania, she would come with him.

Once more the air was full of preparations for departure. The Indians came to Pennsbury to take leave of him. They assured him that they would never break their covenant with him, for, said one, smiting his head three times, it was not made in their heads but, striking his breast, in their hearts.

After a feast which was spread on long tables in the avenue of poplars, the Indians withdrew to an open space near by, built a fire, and danced their cantico around it. Then, sadly, they took the gifts Penn had for them, and vanished into the forest.

A newly elected Assembly met in Philadelphia in September, and this time they managed to agree on a new "charter of privileges." It was much like the old one, based like it on the fundamental principle of religious liberty, but it contained two important changes. Under the old plan, only the Council could propose laws, while the Assembly voted on them. Under the new plan the Assembly could propose laws. The other change was that the Province and the Territories could separate their governments at any time within the next three years provided that they gave due notice. This was a real grief to Penn, who felt that such lack of unity was a kind of failure, but he agreed to it. He signed the new constitution. It was the third that the twenty-year old province had had, but this one lasted until the Revolution.

Then Penn asked the Assembly to nominate a man for deputy-governor during his absence, but they thanked him and refused. He appointed Andrew Hamilton, who had been governor of East and West Jersey, and made James Logan Secretary of the Colony and Clerk of the Council.

Almost everything was done now. He called the inhabitants of Philadelphia together to take formal leave of them, and to give them as an act of his good will a charter. For the last time he went to a meeting for worship, and found there, as he always did, relief from his perplexities and healing for his hurts. There love was unclouded.

Of the departing Governor, Isaac Norris wrote: "The unhappy misunderstandings in some and unwarrantable opposition in others have been a block to our plenary comforts in him and his own quiet; but these are externals only . . . and in this I take a degree of satisfaction after all, that we part in love. . . . His excellent wife . . . has carried under and through all with a wonderfull evenness, humility, and freedom; her sweetness and goodness have become her character and are indeed extraordinary. In short we love her and she deserves it."

On the third of November 1701, the ship *Dalmahoy* sailed. "We had a swift passage; twenty-six days from capes to soundings. . . . Tishe and Johnnie, after the first five days, hearty and well," wrote Penn to James Logan, "and Johnnie exceeding cheerful all the way."

30

Gathering Clouds

P ENN never saw Pennsylvania again, although he hoped always to go back to live at Pennsbury Manor and sail the Delaware in his barge, to eat hominy with the Indians, to walk the wide streets of Philadelphia and see the city grow and thrive around him.

He managed to prevent the bill from coming up before Parliament that would have taken the government of Pennsylvania away from him—and he lived to be sorry that he had upon his shoulders the burden of so difficult and troublesome a colony. The time came when, if he could have sold Pennsylvania to the Crown without selling too the constitution and liberties which he had given to the people, he would thankfully have done it.

For Pennsylvania was suffering all the pains and conflicts that go with rapid growth. The colonists raised too much wheat and could not sell it; feeling poor, they refused to pay their quit-rents. They quarreled among themselves; one group opposed everything that Penn tried to do for them and wrote complaining letters about him to those people in England who would be most glad to make trouble for him. The Territories separated from the Province and called themselves Delaware.

One trouble with the Pennsylvanians was that they did not like the deputy-governors Penn sent. Andrew Hamilton died at the end of a year, and after his death Penn found out that all the time he was governor he had been working secretly against Penn's government with the Lords of Trade and Plantations. Penn, though he was sorely hurt—"I could as soon have picked a pocket or denied my friend or name," he wrote—immediately, in his usual forgiving way, set about helping Hamilton's widow and finding a job for his son.

The next governor he chose was a young man of twenty-six, named John Evans, not a Friend but, Penn thought, "sober and sensible . . . he will be discreet and advisable." Once again he was mistaken in his judgment of character. Young Evans was anything but sober, sensible, discreet, and advisable. He was impossible. His private life was a scandal, his mismanagement of public affairs infuriating. He did one stupid thing after another until the province, finding at last one thing to agree upon, wrote to Penn and asked him to remove Deputy-Governor Evans. This Penn did immediately, but much damage had already been done.

Meanwhile, William and Mary had both died, Mary first and then William, and in 1702 Queen Anne, younger daughter of James II, came to the throne. She was friendly to the Quakers and especially to her father's old friend, William Penn. Now again Penn was lodging in Kensington and doing good works about the court. He tried to save Daniel Defoe, who had at that time not yet written *Robinson Crusoe*, from the pillory, but he did not succeed.

His family was growing. Tommy, "a lovely large child," Hannah, Margaret, Richard, and Dennis, came to join the lively Johnnie. William Junior's beautiful little Gulielma Maria was followed by Springett, "a mere Saracen," according to his grandfather, and William the Third. "We are now Major, Minor, and Minimus," wrote Penn.

Tishe, soon after they came back from Pennsylvania, forgot William Masters (to that gentleman's vast indignation) and married a wealthy widower named William Aubrey, a disagreeable person—a "scraping man," Penn said—who added to Penn's difficulties by clamoring for Tishe's dowry just when money was scarcest.

But William Junior remained the most heart-breaking of his father's problems. While Penn was in Pennsylvania, he had been cutting a swath in London, drinking and spending more money than he had. Penn, who felt that if he had been with the boy during those two crucial years he might have saved him, now paid his debts and decided to send him to America as his representative, hoping that there, removed from his riotous companions and given a little responsibility, he would straighten up and mend his ways.

Penn wrote to the faithful James Logan to keep an eye on Billy. "Go with him to Pennsbury, advise him, contract and recommend his acquaintance. No rambling to New York or mongrel correspondence. He has promised fair. . . . He has wit, kept the top company, and must be handled with love and wisdom."

Later when Billy, after delays, had finally got his passage, Penn wrote: "Watch him, outwit him, and honestly overreach him for his good. Fishings, little journeys (as to see the Indians, etc.) will divert him, and interest Friends to bear all they can. . . . Pennsylvania has cost me dearer in my poor child than all other considerations. . . . I yet hope."

There was to be no rambling to New York, but Billy was to have all the hunting and fishing he wanted. Penn took time in all his affairs to write about Billy's hunting dogs. "If my son sends hounds, as he provides two or three couple of choice ones for deer, foxes, and wolves, pray let great care be taken of them."

Everything was ready; reform was to be made as easy and pleasant as possible for the young man. In just one thing Penn slipped up: Governor Evans. The twenty-six-year-old deputy-governor and Penn's twenty-two-year-old son were soon boon companions, and the worst possible influence on each other.

Before the year was out the two of them got into a disgraceful brawl in a public house and fought with the night-watchmen. After that, William Penn Junior, furious with everybody and everything, shook the dust of Pennsylvania off his feet, resigned from the Society of Friends, which had dared to criticize his conduct, and finally, abandoning his family to his father, went off to

France. "He is my greatest affliction," wrote Penn, "for his soul's and my country's and family's sake."

The second William's extravagance had added its weight to the family burden. In 1707 the financial disaster which had long been hovering like a hawk over Penn's head swooped down. Philip Ford, a Quaker of Bristol, had been for years his trusted agent. When Penn, needing money to go to America, had borrowed twenty-eight hundred pounds from Ford, he gave as his security a mortgage on Pennsylvania. At least he thought it was a mortgage. To his amazement and horror, he now found that the paper which he had signed without properly reading it—fatally unbusinesslike—was not a mortgage but a deed of sale. According to this deed, he had sold Pennsylvania to Philip Ford for twenty-eight hundred pounds and then rented it back from him! Now after Philip Ford the elder died, his widow and son appeared with a bill for fourteen thousand pounds, which they said Penn owed them. Henry Goldney, a Quaker who lived next door to the Gracechurch Street meeting-house, and Herbert Springett, a relative of Gulielma's, who had had legal experience, came to his rescue. They went through all the papers and found that for years the Fords had been systematically cheating Penn. Whenever he sold any land, they had taken the money themselves, as if they owned the land, and then charged him a commission for the sale. By juggling and charging an illegal rate of interest, they had worked up this sum of fourteen thousand pounds, and asserted besides that Pennsylvania was legally theirs by purchase.

Penn proposed arbitration. The Fords refused.

The matter went to chancery, and the court found that the deed was sound and that Penn owed the Fords two thousand pounds for arrears of "rent" for Pennsylvania. His friends advised him not to pay it. In January 1708, coming out of Gracechurch Street Meeting, he was arrested for debt.

From January of that year until December, William Penn, a prisoner for debt, lived in lodgings in the street called the Old Bailey, near the Sessions House where he had been tried in 1670.

He had been in prison before, but in his youth and for high causes. He was old now, and this was sordid and humiliating. Yet he kept his courage and his cheerfulness. Isaac Norris, who had come from Philadelphia to London, said: "The more he is pressed, the more he rises. He seems of a spirit to bear and rub through difficulties and as thou observes his foundation remains."

His rooms were fairly comfortable, and he was able to see his friends and to hold meetings for worship there. His family was at Brentford, on the Thames near London, and his friends were busy in his behalf. The dishonesty of the Fords was brought out into the open, and their petition for a new charter in Pennsylvania was flatly refused by the government. A little frightened, they were willing to compromise. For seven thousand pounds they would wipe the slate clean and give up their claim to Pennsylvania.

Hannah Penn's father, Thomas Callowhill, and other Friends, raised the money, for which they took a mortgage—a real one this time—on Pennsylvania, and in December 1708, Penn was free to leave the Old Bailey.

He had rubbed through. The tide, quietly and imperceptibly at first, had turned. The Pennsylvanians liked the new deputy-governor, Charles Gookin, whom he sent out. When the Assembly was elected in 1710, it was made up entirely of new men; not a single old member kept his seat—and all were friendly to Penn.

He wrote to Pennsylvania, between the election and the Assembly's first session, a strong and fine letter, in which he urged the province to give up their divisions and contentions and to work together to make good use of the freedom and opportunities which it had cost him so much to give them, so that "yet our poor country may be blessed with peace, love, and industry, and we may once more meet good friends and live so to the end, our relation in the truth having but the same true interest."

The colony responded with a rush of the good spirit that was there under all the strain and conflict. The Assembly passed bills to take care of the expenses of government which had fallen so heavily on Penn. They passed a law that he had wanted, laying prohibitive taxes on the importation of slaves (which the Crown unfortunately vetoed). People settled down to pull together as

Penn had always hoped and expected that they would.

The Penns moved to a large and pleasant house at Ruscombe in Berkshire, and the money which Friends had lent Penn in his need was gradually paid off.

Penn was writing again now; letters as always, some biographical sketches, a preface to the journal of an old friend of his. He dictated to a secretary, walking up and down the room, tapping his cane on the floor for emphasis, and breaking off now and then to settle little matters that people brought to him.

With his writing, and the Friends' meeting at Reading near by, with his gardens and a house full of children, Penn was happy and at peace at last.

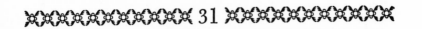

31

Victory

BUT the years of struggle, of anxiety and disappointment and defeat, had broken him. In 1712 he was
stricken with paralysis, and from then until 1718 when
he died, though he kept to the last "a clear soul and a
light heart," his memory was gone, and it was Hannah
Penn, practical and courageous and sweet, who was the
head of the family.

William Penn was buried at Jordans, where the graves
of the Peningtons and Gulielma and the three babies who
died at Rickmansworth lay in the shade of great trees
near a serene little red-brick meeting-house.

The Friends of Reading wrote of him: "In fine, he
was learned without vanity; apt without forwardness;
facetious in conversation yet weighty and serious—of an
extraordinary greatness of mind, yet void of the stain of
ambition; as free from rigid gravity as he was clear of
unseemly levity; a man, a scholar, a friend; a minister
surpassing in speculative endowments, whose memorial
will be valued by the wise and blessed with the just."

Far away in Pennsylvania, the Indians, mourning for
Onas whom they loved, sent to Hannah Penn skins to

make a garment suitable for traveling through a thorny wilderness without her guide.

So troubled had been his last years, so beset with difficulties, that to some who lived in his own time it might have seemed that he went down in defeat. But he never sought success for himself, only for the ideas for which he spent his life. Here he was victorious. The little boy who heard God speak in his own heart grew up to send word from the Tower of London: "My prison shall be my grave before I will budge a jot, for I owe my conscience to no mortal man." And today the religious liberty for which he struggled and suffered we take for granted as part of our inheritance. The tall young man who inspired twelve ordinary earnest citizens to take a stand that established for all time the sacredness of trial by jury became the farsighted statesman who went unarmed and unafraid among the Indians and made friends with them, who built a great state on liberty in religion and democracy in government. Today the constitution of the United States shows the influence of Penn's first charter for Pennsylvania. The harassed and hunted friend of a deposed king looked beyond his own troublous concerns and made a plan for peace in Europe based on the principle that "the truest means to peace is justice, not war." But there the world has not yet caught up with William Penn.

APPENDIX

Selected List of Authorities[*]

BY PENN

From Penn's *Works*, London, 1726, vols. I, II.
  "Advice to His Children."
  "The Sandy Foundation Shaken."
  "The Great Case of Liberty of Conscience."
  "Letter to Mary Pennyman."
  "Truth Exalted."
  "Truth Rescued from Imposture."
  "Letter of Love to the Young Convinced."
  "The People's Ancient and Just Liberties Asserted in
    the Trial of William Penn and William Mead at
    the Sessions Held at the Old Bailey."
  "No Cross, No Crown."
  "Travels in Holland and Germany."
  "New Witnesses Proved Old Hereticks."
  "Judas and the Jews."
The Peace of Europe, Some Fruits of Solitude, and Other Writings, New York, Dutton (Everyman's Library).
"Journal of Penn's Nine Months in Ireland," from *Pennsylvania Magazine of History and Biography*, vol. XL.

---

[*] For complete bibliography, up to 1932, see: Mary Kirk
Spence, *William Penn: a Bibliography*, Pennsylvania Historical
Commission, Harrisburg, 1932, Bulletin No. 1.

ABOUT PENN

An Account of the Convincement of Wm. Penn, delivered by himself to Thomas Harvey about thirty years since, which Thomas Harvey related to me in a brief manner as well as his memory would serve after such a difference of time. 1729. (Manuscript in Friends House Library, Euston Road, London.)

Besse, Joseph, *An Account of the Author's Life*, prefixed to the first edition of Penn's *Works*, London, 1726.

Brailsford, Mabel, *The Making of William Penn*, New York, 1930.

Buck, William Joseph, *William Penn in America*, Philadelphia, 1888.

Clarkson, Thomas, *Memoirs of the Private and Publick Life of William Penn*, 2 vols., London, 1813.

Dixon, William Hepworth, *History of William Penn, Founder of Pennsylvania*, London, 1872.

Dobrée, Bonamy, *William Penn, Quaker and Pioneer*, London, 1932.

Graham, John William, *William Penn, Founder of Pennsylvania*, New York, 1916.

Hull, William I., *Topical Biography of William Penn*, New York, Oxford Press, 1937.

Hull, William I., *William Penn and the Dutch Quaker Migration to Pennsylvania*, Swarthmore, Pennsylvania, 1935.

Janney, Samuel M., *Life of William Penn with Selections from His Correspondence and Autobiography*, Philadelphia, 1852.

Jenkins, Howard M., *The Family of William Penn*, Philadelphia, 1899.

Myers, Albert Cook, *William Penn, His Own Account of the Indians, 1683*, Philadelphia, 1935.

Myers, Albert Cook, *William Penn's Early Life in Brief*, Moylan, Pennsylvania, 1937.

Penn, Granville, *Memorials of Sir William Penn*, 2 vols., London, 1833.

Pound, Arthur, *The Penns of Pennsylvania and England*, New York, 1932.

Rigg, J. M., Article on Penn in the *Dictionary of National Biography*.

Webb, Maria, *Penns and Peningtons of the Seventeenth Century*, London, 1867.

ABOUT PENN'S TIMES

Braithwaite, William Charles, *The Beginnings of Quakerism*, London, 1912.

Braithwaite, William Charles, *Second Period of Quakerism*, London, 1919.

Croese, Gerard, *The General History of the Quakers*, London, 1696.

Dictionary of National Biography, Articles on Sidney, Locke, Ormonde, Ossory, Orrery, Sunderland, Charles II, and James II.

Ellwood, Thomas, *Life of Thomas Ellwood by His Own Hand*, New York, 1900.

Evelyn, John, *Memoirs Illustrative of the Life and Writings of John Evelyn, Comprising his Diary for 1641 to 1705–06, and a Selection of His Familiar Letters*, edited by William Bray, London, 1818.

Fox, George, *Journal*, edited by Norman Penny, 2 vols., Cambridge, 1911.

Fox, George, *Short Journal and Itinerary Journals*, edited by Norman Penny, Cambridge, 1925.

Friends Historical Society, London, *Journal* (scattered material).

Friends Historical Society of Pennsylvania, *Bulletin* (scattered material).

Gordon, Charles, *The Old Bailey and Newgate*, New York, n.d.

Hazard, Samuel, *Annals of Pennsylvania*, Philadelphia, 1850.

Pennsylvania Historical Society, *Memoirs* (scattered material).

Pennsylvania Historical Society, *Pennsylvania Magazine of History and Biography* (scattered material).

Pepys, Samuel, *Diary*, 8 vols., London, 1920.

Robinson, Ralph M., *The Penn Country and the Chilterns*, London, 1929.

Rutty, John, *History of the Rise and Progress of the People Called Quakers in Ireland*, Dublin, 1751.

Sewel, William, *History of the Rise, Increase, and Progress of the Christian People Called Quakers*, London, 1725.

Sharpless, Isaac, *A Quaker Experiment in Government*, Philadelphia, 1898.

Story, Thomas, *A Journal of the Life of Thomas Story*, Newcastle, 1742.

Summers, W. H., *Memories of Jordans and the Chalfonts, and the Early Friends in the Chiltern Hundreds*, London, 1895.

Trevelyan, George Macaulay, *England under the Stuarts*, New York, 1905.

Victoria History of the Counties of England, vol. II, Essex.

Walford, Edward, *Old and New London*, 6 vols., London, n.d.

Watson, John F., *Annals of Philadelphia*, Philadelphia, 1830.

Wood, Anthony, *Athenæ Oxoniensis*, vols. I, II, IV.

Index

25 400WNC FM 6052
12/93 39255